Cambridge
with Kids
Pocket Guide

Includes Ely, Huntingdon, Newmarket, Peterborough and St Ives

1st Edition

By Katie Higney

Cambridge with Kids: Pocket Guide 1st Edition

www.cambridgewithkids.com

Published by Red Cherry Books
April 2015
www.redcherrybooks.com

Cover Design & Photography by Red Cherry Books
ISBN 978-0-9928010-6-9
Copyright © Katie Higney
All rights reserved.

The information is up to date at the time of printing, but occasionally contact details, opening times or other details can change or become outdated, or for inadvertent errors or omissions. Please always confirm information before setting out. It is up to parents to decide whether the information given in 'Cambridge with Kids' is suitable or appropriate for their children.

Disclaimer
The author has taken every care in compiling information and material for this book. The author will not be held responsible for any loss, injury, illness, damage or inconvenience caused as a result of advice, information or inaccuracy or error contained in these pages.

Copyright

Maps
Contains Ordnance Survey data © Crown Copyright and database right 2015 used under the OS OpenData license. Also contains © OpenStreetMap data available under the Open Database License www.ordnancesurvey.co.uk/business-and-government www.openstreetmap.org/copyright

RED CHERRY BOOKS
81 Fernwalk, Ballincollig,
Cork, Ireland

Contents

Days out, Ideas, Fun!

I spent several years in Cambridge with children and I thought it would be great to have all the information in one place. After all, being a parent is a busy job!

Whether you live here, or are just visiting, this guide will provide you with all the information you'll need to explore the city and beyond. *www.cambridgewithkids.com*

1

Cambridge City

The city is best known for its colleges, the tourists, students and bikes. However it is not merely a city with a historic past, or just a town with a famous University. It is a great place for children, with fantastic parks, interesting museums and events.

Most locals get around by bike. You can even cycle to the centre of town and borrow a buggy for the day. Alternatively, buses are frequent, have low floors and buggy access.

There are playgrounds in most areas and also right in the centre of town at Christ's Pieces and Jesus Green.

It is a beautiful city to walk around. The 'Backs' are covered in bright yellow daffodils in the Spring. Here you can see the spires of Kings College and pretty bridges over the Cam. You can enjoy the simple pleasure of having an ice cream with the kids on a hot day by the river, watching the people float by in the punts.

If it is raining, you could get a kids activity pack to explore the Fitzwilliam Museum, or see a movie at the reduced price Saturday morning cinemas.

There are five theatres, three cinemas and plenty of indoor play centres so there is always something to do.

Top 10 Family Favourites

1 **Museums** Find the Knights in Armour in the Fitzwilliam Museum in Cambridge; find out about the voyages of Captain Cook at the Museum of Archaeology and Anthropology (p40) or see the light shine through the stained glass at the 12th century Ely Cathedral (p116).

2 **Summer swims** Splash about in an outdoor pool in the summer, in Jesus Green or Lammas Land, right in the heart of Cambridge. Both are by the river, both have kiosks for snacks and big stretches of grass, with playgrounds (p49).

3 **Country parks** Wandlebury Country Park, with it's historic Iron Age Hillfort; Milton Country Park; Paxton Pits and Ferry Meadows. The Georgian Wimpole Hall Estate and the impressive mansion of Audley End with landscapes by Capability Brown have regular family events (p108).

4 **Visit an air show** Watch the magnificent World War planes zoom across the sky at the Imperial War Museum, Duxford. It has regular weekends such as the Flying Legends' and the Battle of Britain (p102).

5 **Seasonal fun** Visit the Lambs at Easter in Wimpole Hall (p113); a summer picnic in Grantchester Meadows (p69; get lost in Autumn at the Milton Maize Maze (p125); see the gardens at Anglesey Abbey in winter (p108). The Cambridge University Botanic Garden is well worth a visit all year round (p13).

6 **Saturday Movies** The local cinemas have a low cost Kids Saturday club for young children. There are three in Cambridge: the Arts Picturehouse; the Vue Cinema and Cineworld (p48). There are also 'Big Scream' Wednesdays, where adults can watch a movie with babies under one years old. There are toddler time movies and autism friendly screenings.

7 **Take a train or bus for an adventure** The train to Ely only takes 20 minutes – visit the Cathedral and park (p116); Or try the guided bus to St Ives (p119) or bus to Newmarket (p118) or Huntingdon (p117). You could also hop on board the miniature railway at Audley End (p102).

8 **Play tennis or football** outside on the many open green spaces (p11). Many have short grass such as Parker's Piece which is where the rules of football were invented. These are great to run around in. In the summer there are outdoor table tennis tables in Christ's Pieces and free tennis courts.

9 **Go on a Treasure Hunt** left behind on a trail with geocache (p87). You could look for wildlife, see if you can spot butterflies, dragonflies, birds and insects in the local nature reserves (p12). Hunt the streets of Cambridge for animal sculptures, like the Mammoth and Iguanadon in Downing Street (p80).

10 **Indoor Fun** There is plenty to do if it is raining. You could go swimming at the great local pools such as Parkside, or tumble about in the indoor soft play areas. Try archery, volleyball or football inside at the Kelsey Kerridge Sports Hall (p49).

Top City Sights

Days Out

Fun for Free

Top Events *124*

Top City Green Spaces 11

Botanic Gardens - *lake, greenhouse, cafe, plants*
Christ's Pieces - *central, playground, tennis*
Jesus Green - *summer outdoor pool, skateboard ramp, playground, tennis courts, kiosk*
Lammas Land - *outdoor pool, playground, ducks, river.*
Midsummer Common - *to watch the rowers*
Parker's Piece - *for football/frisbee*

Rainy Days

City of Cambridge Map

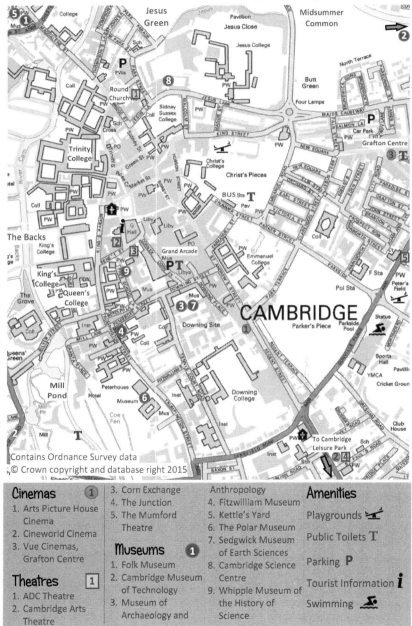

Contains Ordnance Survey data
© Crown copyright and database right 2015

9

Cinemas ①	3. Corn Exchange	Anthropology	Amenities
1. Arts Picture House Cinema	4. The Junction	4. Fitzwilliam Museum	
2. Cineworld Cinema	5. The Mumford Theatre	5. Kettle's Yard	Playgrounds 🛝
3. Vue Cinemas, Grafton Centre		6. The Polar Museum	
	Museums ①	7. Sedgwick Museum of Earth Sciences	Public Toilets T
Theatres 1	1. Folk Museum	8. Cambridge Science Centre	Parking P
1. ADC Theatre	2. Cambridge Museum of Technology	9. Whipple Museum of the History of Science	Tourist Information 𝒊
2. Cambridge Arts Theatre	3. Museum of Archaeology and		Swimming 🏊

Cambridge Green Spaces

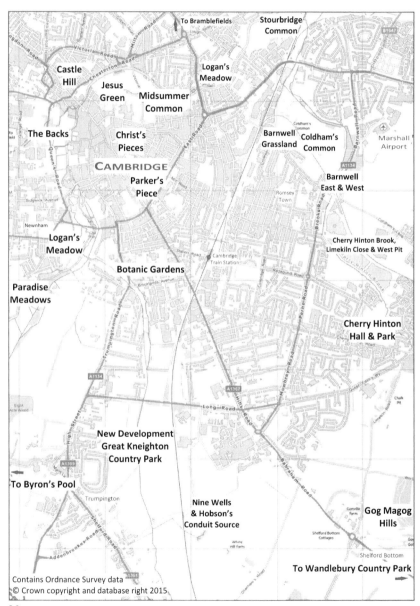

To Bramblefields
Stourbridge Common
Castle Hill
Logan's Meadow
Jesus Green
Midsummer Common
The Backs
Christ's Pieces
Barnwell Grassland
Coldham's Common
Marshall Airport
CAMBRIDGE
Parker's Piece
Barnwell East & West
Newnham
Logan's Meadow
Cherry Hinton Brook, Limekiln Close & West Pit
Botanic Gardens
Cambridge Train Station
Paradise Meadows
Cherry Hinton Hall & Park
New Development Great Kneighton Country Park
To Byron's Pool
Trumpington
Nine Wells & Hobson's Conduit Source
Gog Magog Hills
To Wandlebury Country Park

Contains Ordnance Survey data
© Crown copyright and database right 2015

Arbury
Town Park
Campkin Road

Found behind the Arbury Community Centre. Nearby are the two Kings Hedges Recreation grounds.

Coe Fen
(Also Lammas Land and Sheep's Green)
The Fen Causeway

This is meadow land from the Mill Pond to Lammas Land. It often has cows grazing and follows an old wall at the back of the Fitzwilliam Museum. It has small criss cross paths leading to small bridges over the river.

Coldham's Common
Barnwell Road

This is a very large green in the east of Cambridge, Romsey Town area. It is near Abbey Pool and Coldham's Lane playground. Coldham's Brook runs through it.

Midsummer Common
Chesterton/Newmarket Road

A lovely large, ancient grassland by the river. The grass is rougher and not as good for picnics or football. These are busy and well used footpaths, so keep to the left to let bikes pass. Sometimes it contains a herd of cows, recently Red Poll Bullocks. The University boathouses line one side, and you can watch the rowers train for races. In the past few years, the river has also filled with houseboats. The Fort St. George pub serves food.

Parker's Piece
East Road

This is a popular large, flat green. It is great for playing football and other games. In summer you can watch cricket. It has a public toilet and refreshment kiosk in the corner by the Catholic Church.

The Backs
Queen's Road

The 'Backs' of the riverside colleges have well maintained lawns and in spring are full of daffodils and crocuses beneath the trees. It is more of a walk than a playing space. This is a timeless and very beautiful part of the city.

11

Nature Reserves

Barnwell East & West
This used to be a piggery, but is now grassland, scrub and a small pond. There are wild orchids and even grass snakes.

Bramblefields Chesterton
Scrub, grassland and a small pond. You can find newts, frogs, dragonflies and damselflies.

Byron's Pool
Grantchester
This is on the road from Grantchester to Trumpington. It has several pools and woodland. Lord Byron the poet used to like swimming here.

Limekiln Close & West Pitt
Cherry Hinton
These were chalk quarries, it is now woodland and grassland.

Logan's Meadow Abbey
On the banks of the River Cam, with mature willows and temporary ponds.

Nine Wells
Near Addenbrooks Hospital
This is a pretty beech copse with springs, which are the source for Hobson's Conduit.

Paradise Meadow Newnham
On the beginning of the path to Grantchester from Cambridge, this has woodland, willows and a marsh.

University of Cambridge Botanic Garden

The garden was established as a University teaching and research resource by Professor John Stevens Henslow on land acquired in 1831. It finally opened to the public in 1846.

There are 40 acres of beautiful gardens and greenhouses. There is a lake and rock garden. It has a cafe and picnic area, a lake and woods. There are grey squirrels and foxes. A group of badgers wander at night. Also at dusk the Common Pipistrelle Bats hunt and roost in the tree hollows.

There are frogs and toads which eat the snails and slugs that would otherwise eat the flowers. The only reptile is the grass snake which you can sometimes see swimming in the lake. There is one grass snake which seems to like the Glasshouse Palm House and is known as Hissing Sid!

It is great for younger kids to run around by the trees, look at the ducks and explore the meandering paths.

1 Brookside, Cambridge CB2 1JE
Tel: 01223 336265
www.botanic.cam.ac.uk
Admission: £5 for Adults, 0-16 yrs free
Open: 10am-6pm Apr to Sep;
10 am-5pm Feb, Mar, Oct;
10 am-4 pm Nov to Jan.

Parks with Playgrounds

Alexander Gardens
Carlyle Road
This has a climb net for older children, and a play area for under 6s.

Cherry Hinton Hall Park
Cherry Hinton Road
The park has a lake, two paddling pools, and play equipment for older and young children. Also a bird sanctuary.

Christ's Pieces
Emmanuel Road
A very central park with four free tennis courts, a refreshment kiosk and a popular play area for the under 6s. It is a good rest stop between shops and is right by the bus station. It has flower beds and a popular hang out for teenagers. There is a Princess Diana Memorial Garden in the centre.

Jesus Green
Chesterton Road/Victoria Avenue
This is adjacent to the River Cam, and a great place to watch the ducks and swans. It has a playground for smaller children, a small picnic area and also a skateborard ramp, tennis courts and an open air swimming pool open in the summer. There is also a small kiosk for food or ice creams. It has a beautiful avenue of London Planes and horse chestnut trees. It's a great place to have a picnic.

Lammas Land
The Fen Causeway
This is a lovely place to take the kids. It is by the river, with a playground, and a paddling pool. There is a kiosk in the summer. On the wilder parts across the river from the playground are cows. There are some small streams and weeping willows, one side leads to Grantchester, the other to the Mill Pond. It also has a free tennis court. Probably my favourite park.

Stourbridge Common
Riverside to Fen Road
This is quite scrub like and not good for playing on, but it has a children's playground near the Riverside entrance. You could take a long walk along the River Cam where you can see swans, ducks, houseboats and rowers.

Playgrounds

Arbury Court play area
Older and younger children's area.

Brooks Rd play area
Springy's, a slide and swings suitable for all ages.

Cherry Hinton Rec
Two football pitches, a skateboard ramp and playground.

Chesterton Rec
Two football pitches, skate ramp and under 6's area.

Chestnut Grove Rec
All ages playground.

Coleridge Rec
Football, tennis and children's playground.

Dudly Rd Rec
Skate ramp and playground.

Flower Street
Swing and slide.

Green End Rec
Youth shelter, playground.

Gunhild Close
Playground. Timber goals.

Histon Rd Rec
Good children's play area with slide and swings.

Holbrook Rd Rec
Goal end, climber, and springy's.

Kings Hedges Rec

Children's playground and a learner pool.

Riverside and Newmarket Rd
Large open space that leads you right out into the country following the river. Good children's playground near Stanley Road entrance. Cows and horses graze on the land here.

Petersfield play area

Peverel Rd

Ravensworth Gardens

Riley Way

Mill Rd/East Rd corner

Romsey Rec

Scotland Rd

Shelly Row

St Albans Rd
Football pitch, skateboard ramp and playground.

St Matthew's Piece

St Thomas Square

Tenby Close

Tennison Rd/Ravensworth Gardens This is on a roof garden.

Thorpe Way/Fison Rd
Trim trail for small children and fitness zones for older children.

Trumpington Rec
Football pitch and playground.

Woodhead Drive

Top 10 Touristy Things to do with Kids

1. Walk up to the top of **Great St. Mary's Church.** The view over Cambridge is worth the steep climb, but try not to be on the stairs when the bells ring!

2. Visit the **Fitzwilliam Museum.** A very fine museum with a grand entrance, knight's armour, cafe and plenty for kids to do.

3. Walk along **the Backs** of King's College in the snow or spring.

4. Take a picnic by the **Mill Pond** and watch people punt by.

5. Visit the **Botanic Gardens** and run around the trees.

6. Play football in **Parker's Piece**, where football association rules were created. There is a kiosk and public toilets and Parkside swimming pool near here.

7. **Trinity College**, Chapel and Gardens, Clare, Queen's or Downing College. Take a peek at the courtyards, the history, and the inspiring work of it's past and current students.

8. Get a cake or a bun from **Fitzbillies Cake Shop.** Delicious!

9. Spot the Knights Templar at the **Round Church.** Although be warned, this medieval church is right opposite a sweet shop with just about every confectionary that you can think of!

10. Run up the very steep **Castle Hill,** next to the County Council offices. Imagine being a Roman or Saxon, and see the views.

A Kid Friendly Guide to the Colleges

The University of Cambridge is the third oldest university in the world (after Bologna and Oxford), founded 1209. It was formed in the 13th Century by a group of students who fled from hostility in Oxford.

The earliest college was Peterhouse, founded in 1284. There are now 31 colleges and over 150 departments, faculties and schools. Cambridge has produced 89 Nobel Prizes, the most of any university in the world.

If you are visiting Cambridge, then seeing the colleges may be on top of your list. If you live in Cambridge, it can be a nice change to walk around the colleges, and a good way to combine local highlights with visitors or grandparents who come to visit. Although be warned it gets very busy in the summer. I think the best time to visit is in the quieter months of winter or early spring.

Admission

You can visit some for free, others for an admission fee. Walking on the lawns, or games or picnics, exploring stairs or other places is not allowed, so be mindful with children. The colleges are private places where people live, work and study, so it isn't a great place to be noisy or let the kids run riot. But as a Harry Potter type experience, it can be fun to wander through the courts, chapels and halls.

During the examination time from mid-April to late June most colleges are closed to the public. Some colleges do not admit prams, dogs or push-chairs. Information about these restrictions are given on notice boards and at the college gates.

Alternatively, you do not have to go into the colleges to enjoy them. You could walk along the backs of the colleges. Start from the Round Church, past Trinity College, turn right into Free School Lane, over the bridge and around the back of King's College and finish up by the Mill Pond. Here you can get an ice cream or take a picnic and sit watching the punts go by in the Summer.

King's College and King's College Chapel (1441)

This is the most famous and most visited college. I love the architecture, it is big and exalting. There are long queues to the televised 'Festival of Nine Lessons and Carols' on Christmas Eve.

It was founded by Henry VI (who also founded Eton College). However the War of the Roses and lack of money meant that it was not finished until Henry VIIIs reign. You can see the difference in light and dark stone on the chapel's side, where work had to stop and start.

King's College Chapel is one of the best examples of Gothic architecture in Britain. It has 26 soaring stained glass windows and a

Rubens painting 'Adoration of the Magi' behind the chapel altar. Members of the college originally came only from Eton. They did not have to pass their BA degree to become a fellow, where all those not studying astronomy, law or medicine had to take Holy Orders and become priests, or be ejected by the college. In 1851 these rules were changed, and it now often has the highest proportion of students from state schools.

James Gibbs completed the courtyard in 1724. Around 130,000 books are held in the library. Alan Turing (mathematician), John Keynes (economist) and E. M. Forster (novelist) were all students here.

King's Parade, Cambridge
Open: During term time: Mon 9.45am–3.30pm; Tues–Fri 9.30am–3.30pm; Sat 9.30am–3.15pm; Sun 1.15–2.30pm. Out of term: Mon 9.45am–4.30pm; Tues–Sun 9.30am–4.30pm
Admission: Adult £7.50; concessions £5.

Queens' College

Founded by two Queen's in the mid 1400s, the college is linked by the world famous Mathematical Bridge. There is a magnificent medieval Old Hall.

The badge of the college has a wild boar's head, which was the badge of King Richard III. His wife, Anne Neville was a college patron.

The Old Court was built by Reginald Ely, a master mason. The Old Llibrary houses nearly 20,000 manuscripts and books. It also contains a very old celestial globe. Walnut Tree Court was completed in 1616. And indeed there is a Walnut Tree in the square.

The Mathematical Bridge is rumoured to have been built by Sir Isaac Newton without using any nuts or bolts. It is said, in the past ambitious students tried to take the bridge apart to find out. Supposedly they couldn't put it back together again, so had to add nuts and bolts. It is a good story, but not true. The bridge is made of oak by James Essex the Younger in 1749. It decayed and had to be rebuilt in 1905, although teak instead of oak was used. A hand rail was added to

help the Queen Mother cross when she visited.

Students call the older side of the bridge, the 'dark side', and the newer, the 'light Side'. It has a reputation for being a more relaxed and open college, with strong sports, music and drama support.

Notable past students include Erasmus (humanist theologian), Stephen Fry (comedian) and Lord Falconer (former Lord Chancellor).

Silver Street, Cambridge
Open: Mar–Sep 10am–4.30pm; Sep–Nov Mon–Fri 2–4pm, Sat–Sun; 10am–4.30pm; Nov–Mar 2–4pm.. *The President's Lodge, the Old Library, the War Memorial Library, Cripps Dining Hall, staircases and the Fellow's Garden are not open to visitors.*
Admission: £3 per visitor, under 10 free.

Trinity College

This is the richest college in Cambridge and Oxford Universities combined, with a landholding worth £800 million.

This makes it one of the wealthiest estate owners in the UK (behind the Crown Estate, the National Trust and the Church of England). The lands owned are as diverse as the Port of Felixstowe, the O2 Arena, half of Tescos and the Cambridge Science Park. The annual rent is over £20 million.

Did You Know?

The University of Cambridge was founded in 1209.
The library has 29 million books.
The whole town north of the river was almost
wiped out by the Black Death in 1349.
The University of Cambridge has its own constabulary.
There are around 30,000 students in Cambridge.

800 Years Old

The University of Cambridge celebrated its 800th birthday in 2009. It is the second oldest University in the English speaking world. In 1231 it received a charter from King Henry III to teach and govern itself.

It is particularly renowned for maths and science. Charles Babbage designed the world's first computer here in the mid 1800s. It has produced 13 British prime ministers, nine archbishops of Canterbury, and several well known comedians. 90 Nobel laureates have been affiliated to the University in some way.

It has 31 colleges and over 100 academic departments organised into six schools. The colleges are self-governing. In the year ended 31 July 2014, the university had a total income of £1.51 billion. There is a research partnership with MIT in the United States, the Cambridge–MIT Institute. The Cambridge University Press is the oldest printer and publisher in the world.

It is part of the "'golden triangle" of top English universities. It's presence has attracted over 40,000 jobs to the area in the last 50 years, mainly due to the growth of over 1,500 now technological companies based here, part of the "Silicon Fen".

Peterhouse is the first college, founded in 1284 by Hugh Balsham, Bishop of Ely. The first colleges for women were Girton College in 1869 (founded by Emily Davies) and Newnham College in 1872.

The library is designed by Christopher Wren. It contains two Shakespeare folios and letters by Isaac Newton. The Great Court is where Harold Abrahams ran around the College Courtyard in the time it took for the clock to stirke 12. This was a scene shown in the movie Chariots of Fire.

Thomas Nevile, Master of Trinity in 1593, rebuilt much of the college,

including the Great Court and Nevile's Court. The Great Gate has a statue of it's founder, Henry VIII. He holds a table leg in his hand instead of a sword. No-one knows when this was switched. The first astronomical observatory in the University was built on top of the gate, in 1704.

There are lots of tales about this college. Lord Byron kept a pet bear when he was a student here. Another tale is that Trinity is the inventor of an English version of creme brulee, 'Trinity burnt cream'.

The college is a rival of St John's and is reportedly why there is no 'J' on the alphabetical staircases. There are two small cannons on the bowling green also pointed at St John's, although this may be coincidental.

Notable past students include; Isaac Newton, Charles Babbage, Francis Bacon and Jawaharial Nehru. There is a large tree in New Court that some say bore the apples the fell on Newton's head. However it is a chestnut tree, so no apples here.

Trinity has the most Nobel Prize winners. In the 20th Century, 32 were won by members of the colleges and five field medals in mathematics. Prince Charles obtained a lower second degree here in 1970. He still retains a private room at the back of the college for visits.

There are lovely lime and cherry trees lining the Avenue on the back entrance to Queen's Road.

Trinity Street, Cambridge
Open: Winter time 10am–4pm (last entry 3.30pm)
Summer time 10am–5pm (last entry 4.30pm)

Admission: Adult £1; children £0.50 (children under 12 free)

St. John's College and the School of Pythagoras

A beautiful college, which has a large number of courtyards. The School of Pythagoras is the oldest academic building in Cambridge. Wordsworth had a room here. The lovely 'Bridge of Sighs' links the college. It was founded by the Lady Margaret Beaufort and has produced three Archbishops, nine Nobel Prize winners and six Prime Ministers. The original site was the hospital of St John. Now it has a huge Great Gate in red and white brick, with the Red Rose of Lancaster and Portcullis emblems of the founder.

The college arms has mythical beasts with elephants tails, antelopes bodies, goats heads and horns called Yales. At the top is St John the Evangelist, with a poisoned chalice in his hand and an eagle at his feet.

Fellows of the college are the only people outside the Royal Family legally allowed to eat unmarked mute swans. There are also said to be a number of ghosts. Some were 'exorcised' in the 1700s by being shot at. The college is supposedly haunted by the ghost of a student James Wood, who was so poor he couldn't afford to

light his room and would work in the stairway. Another mystery is the clock tower, it has four blank clock faces and no clock and no one knows why.

The Chapel is the tallest building in Cambridge. The dining hall is magnificent, with black and gold beams in the ceiling. Queen Elizabeth rode into the hall on horseback in 1564. That must have been quite a sight to behold!

The second court has been called the finest Tudor court in Engalnd. Part of the D Day landings were planned from here. The limestone Wren Bridge and beautiful Bridge of Sighs are both part of the college. The latter is a neo-gothic covered footwalk designed by Henry Hutchinson.

The School of Pythagoras, built 1200 approx was originally a private house of the Merton family. It is now used as a drama space. The Cripps building is a 1960s

construction, to house the increasing numbers of students.

St John's Street, Cambridge
Open: Mar–Oct 10am–5pm; Nov–Feb 10am–3.30pm
Admission: Adult £5; concessions £3.50; children under 12 free

Jesus College (1496)

This is a large college with attractive grounds and many sculptures. It's full name is 'The College of the Blessed Virgin Mary, Saint John the Evangelist and the glorious Virgin Saint Radegund', but that is a bit of a mouthful. The cockerel is the college symbol, after it's founder John Alcock, Bishop of Ely.

The buildings were originally a Nunnery. The Chapel, founded in 1157, is the oldest buidling in Cambridge still in use. Thomas Cranmer was a notable figure, he published the Book of Common Prayer. He attended the college at the age of 14, and became the first Protestant Archbishop of Canterbury. Samuel Coleridge (English Romantic Poet) Prince Edward and Nick Hornby (novelist) were also previous students here.

Jesus Lane, Cambridge
Open: 9am–6pm
Free

Christ's College (1505)

This has educated some of the most renowned alumni, including

Charles Darwin and John Milton. The bottom of the gate has been cut off to accomodate a rise in street level. It has lovely wisteria in the spring on the Master's Lodge. The modern tiered concrete New Court building has been called 'the Typewriter'. It also has the oldest outdoor pool in Europe (closed to visitors).

St Andrew's Street, Cambridge
Open: 9am–4pm. *The Fellows' Garden is open Mon–Fri only.*
Free

Clare College (1326)

Clare is known for its chapel choir and lovely gardens on 'the Backs'. It has some fine classicist and gothic architecture. It is known as a liberal and progressive college, and very musical. Clare Bridge is the oldest in Cambridge, with fourteen stone balls, one missing a section. Some say that the original builder wasn't paid the full amount for his work and so he removed a segment!

Trinity Lane, Cambridge
Open: Opening times vary. When open, the Fellows' and Scholars' gardens, Chapel and Hall can be visited Mon–Sun 10.45am–4.15pm.
During term time, visits to the gardens are by special arrangement only.
Easter weekend and Jul–Sep
Admission: £3 (discounted rate of £2 for groups 10+)

Corpus Christi College (1352)

'The College of Corpus Christi and the Blessed Virgin Mary' is the only college founded by Cambridge townspeople. The college is particularly rich in silver. The guild of Corpus Christi was founded in 1349 in response to the Black Death here. They bought lands and their patron, the Duke of Lancaster applied to King Edward III for a license to found a new college. The Corpus Christi procession used to be a parade through the streets to Magdelene Bridge, until the English Reformation ended this in 1535. However the college still retains part of this as a grand dinner on the feast day of Corpus Christi, the Thursday after Trinity Sunday.

This has always been a strongly clerical college. The Archbishop Matthew Parker is the greatest benefactor of the college, and gave it the symbol of the pelican. He ensured the safety of the library books and silver, by saying that if more than a certain amount were lost the whole collection would pass to Gonville & Caius College. That is the reason that the college retains its whole collection of silver and books. The phrase *'Nosey Parker'* came from the Archbishops

---

Residents' Cards

These are available to gain entry to King's College and other colleges and are valid for three years. They cost £10 to cover costs, and you can fill out the form online if you live within a 12 mile radius of Great St Mary's Church. Children under 18 do not need a card, but must be accompanied by an adult with a card. You will need a passport style digital photo.
www.kings.cam.ac.uk/visit/residents

---

assiduous nature in obtaining books.

Corpus owns the **Eagle Pub**, managed by Greene King, nearby. This is where Watson and Crick, excited, ran into the pub and declared:
"We have found the secret of life!"
and presumably sat down for a well deserved pint. They both worked at the Cavendish Laboratory, where they had discovered the structure of DNA.

Trumpington Street, Cambridge
Jan–Apr 2–4pm; Jul–Sep
Open: 10.30am–4.30pm; Oct–Dec 2–4pm
Admission: £2.50

Downing College (1800)

Sir George Downing, whose grandfather built 10 Downing Street, used his inheritance to found the college. The grand entrance was designed by William Wilkins in the neo classical style. It is a politically active college, and known for medicine and law. The college boat club has often won the 'Lent Bumps'. John Cleese and Sir John Pendry (physicist) were former students.

Regent Street, Cambridge
Open: 9am–5pm
Free

Emmanuel College (1584)

The college was founded by Walter Mildmay, Chancellor of the

Exchequer to Elizabeth I. The site was originally a Dominican friary until the monasteries were dissolved in King Henry VIIIs reign, 45 years earlier. The chapel was designed by Christopher Wren.

There is a large fish pond in the grounds, and a bathing pool, both originating from the friary.

Harvard University in the USA is modelled on Emmanuel, and founded by an Emmanuel graduate John Harvard.

St Andrew's Street, Cambridge
Open: 9am–6pm
Free

Girton College (1869)

It is one of England's first residential colleges for women, and is still governed by a Mistress.

The main college site is on the outskirts of Giron village, 2.5 miles north of the town. It has fostered equality, keeping a balanced male/female ratio and equal access admittance schemes. It also encourages music. Arianna Huffington, of the Huffington Post was a student here.

Huntingdon Road, Cambridge
Open: 9am–5pm
Free

Gonville & Caius College (1348)

This has a reputation for medicine, with previous students being John Caius, Francis Crick and James Watson (discovery of DNA). Sir Howard Forey (the developer of penicilin) and James Chadwick (the discover of the neutron) were also former students. Stephen Hawking is a current fellow of the college. The college is said to have rights to much of the land in Cambridge.

Harvey, Glisson and Gresham Road were named after alumni of the college.

John Caius, Master from 1559, revived the college's ailing state, but was a bit eccentric. He insisted that no students were admitted who were:
"deformed, dumb, blind, lame, maimed, mutilated, a Welshman, or suffering from any grave or contagious illness, or an invalid that is sick in a serious measure."

There are three gates here symbolising the path of academic life; the Gate of Humility; the Gate of Virtue and finally the Gate of Honour when members have achieved their degrees.

It is a very traditional college, insisting that members attend communal dinners. On the wall of the Hall hangs a college flag that was flown in the South Pole by Edward Wilson in 1912.

Trinity Street, Cambridge
Open: 9am–2pm. *Closed for two weeks in August.*
Free

Magdalene College (1428)

Pronounced 'Maudlin', it began life as a Benedictine hostel. Some of the wealthiest benefactors include the Duke of Norfolk and the Duke of Buckingham. However much of the work building the college was by Thomas Audley, Lord Chancellor for Henry VIII. He donated 7 acres of land in Aldgate, London to the college, which was his reward from Henry VIII for getting rid of Anne Boleyn. However this was taken back illegally by the Crown in 1574 through the banker Benedict Spinola. A gargoyle of Spinola spitting water into the Cam was installed in 1989. Obviously a treachery not forgotten!

It is also a very traditional place, with candlelit formal hall every evening, and the last to admit women (1988). Most of the buildings are in brick rather than stone like other colleges. It is at the foot of Castle Hill, deliberately so that the Monks were not near to the temptations of the town. Samuel Pepys donated his papers and books here upon his death, and are now in the Pepys Building.

A former Master of the college, Peter Peckard 1781, spoke out strongly against the slave trade and achieved for the college a reputation for informed thinking. There are 20 inscriptions in the building of Benson court by another influential literary Master, A. Benson. He wrote the lyrics for Land of Hope and Glory. Mallory Court is named after George Mallory who climbed

Mount Everest *'because it was there'*. The Fellow's Garden includes Monk's Walk, a raised footpath which was once a Roman era floor barrier. The garden used to have several fish ponds however these are all filled in. There are black poplars, quince, plum and cherry trees. It is beautiful in spring.

Magdalene Street, Cambridge
Open: 6am–6pm. *The Pepys Library is open to visitors for limited hours during term and the summer.*
Free

Pembroke College (1347)

William Pitt, the British Prime Minister attended this college. The current master is Sir Richard Dearlove, previously head of the Secret Intelligence Service.

King Edward III granted Marie De St Pol, (the widow of the Earl of Pembroke), the license to found this college on Christmas Eve 1347. It gave preference to students born in France and strongly discouraged excessive drinking.

The gardens are very well kept, and have a bowling green, Plane trees and an 'Orchard' which is now a semi wild ground. The graduates are called 'Valencians' after the original name of the college. The chapel is the first completed work of Sir Christopher

Wren in the classical style. It records the names of the 450 Pembroke men who fell in World War I and II.

Several comedians, Peter Cook, Clive James and Bill Oddie were once 'Pembroke Players', the colleges dramatic society.

Trumpington Street, Cambridge
Open: Open all year round. Tourist groups above the size of a family can visit the College's courts and gardens 2–5pm. The Wren Chapel is open 9am–6pm.
Free

Peterhouse (1284)

The oldest Cambridge college, founded by Hugo de Balsham, the Bishop of Ely. It was granted its charter by King Edward I. It is also a very traditional college, with formal dinings and has a very small student intake.

The buildings have been altered significantly over the years.
It was also the second building in the country to get electric lighting, (the first being the Palace of Wesminister). Andrew Perne, a former master, built the library. The stained glass windows in the dining

hall are Pre-Raphaelite pieces including William Morris.

Michael Portillo and Michael Howard were previous students here, leading the college to have a Conservative reputation.

The grounds south of Gisborne Court have been known as Deer Park from the 19th century. Unfortunately the original deer fell sick after the First World War and are now gone.

Trumpington Street, Cambridge
Open: 9am–5pm
Free

MATHS, TRIPOS AND THE WOODEN SPOON

From the 17th century, since Isaac Newton there has been a strong emphasis on maths, particularly mathematical physics. The exam is known as a Tripos, and students who complete this are called wranglers, the top student being the Senior Wrangler.

In the past, the lowest scorer on the exam was given a huge wooden spoon (1m long, with an oar blade for a handle). The last of these spoons was awarded in 1909 to Cuthbert Lempriere Holthouse. It is kept at Selwym College library.

CAMBRIDGE APOSTLES

This is a discussion group held once a week, and started in 1820 by George Tomlinson, a Cambridge student who became the first Bishop of Gibraltar.

It is an intellectual secret society. The members take turns in hosting the nights, usually weekly, where there is a topic for debate. The hosts provide coffee and sardines on toast, called 'whales'.

They gave rise to the Bloomsbury group, including John Keynes and E.M. Forster. It gained notiority following the exposure of the Cambridge KGB spy ring in 1951, one of whom was an apostle.

Churches

Our Lady and the English Martyrs Church (Roman Catholic)

Hills Road, Cambridge
A beautiful church built in 1890, in neo-gothic style with a 214 foot spire. In 1941 in an air raid, a bomb struck the sacristy. The stained class windows show scenes from the lives of English martyres, such as St John Fisher.

The Round Church

Also 'The Church of the Holy Sepulchre', located opposite the sweet shop on the corner of Rounch Church Street and Bridge Street. It is one of four medieval round churches still in use in England. It was built around 1130, by the Fraternity of the Holy Sepulchre. It has dog tooth ornamentation and carved human heads. There are links with the Knights Templar.

Great St. Mary's Church

King's Parade, Cambridge.
A strongly University Church, built around 1300. In the middle ages it was an official gathering place for meetings and de-bates for the Universi-ty. You can climb the steep winding stairs for a spectacular view of Cambridge. Just try not to be on the stairs when the bell rings!

Sightseeing and Tours

Cambridge Tourist Information Centre

Conducts city tours, has information on local sites.

Peas Hill, Cambridge CB2 3AD
All enquiries: 0871 226 8006
info@visitcambridge.org
www.visitcambridge.org
Open: Summer (Apr-Oct) MonFri 1000-1700, Sat 1000-1700, Sun & Bank Holidays 1100-1500.
Winter (Nov-Mar) Mon-Fri 1000-1700
Sat 1000-1700 Sun - closed

Bus Tours:

City Sightseeing

www.city-sightseeing.com
Cambridge City Hop On Hop Off Tour

Boat Tours: Riverboat Georgina

www.georgina.co.uk
One or two-hour cruises

Disability Access

An access guide and map is available at:
www.admin.cam.ac.uk/univ/disability
You may also contact the individual Colleges and Museums in advance. Disabled parking is located in each of the city's car parks and streets. The Tourist Information Centre has more information.

City College Walk

Short: 1.3 miles, 30 minutes
Long: 2 miles, 1 hour

1. Start in **Christs' Pieces** by the main bus station and walk around the corner to  **Emmanuelle College**. The college contains a pond with fishes. Notice the mother and child sculpture on the corner of John Lewis.

2. Then head across to **Downing Street**, past the **University Archeological and Zoology Museums.** Look up to your left at the carvings of the Mammoth, Iguanadon and the Giant Sloth. There is also a carving of a green man, with leaves coming from his mouth.

3. Carry on down Pembroke Street, and then turn right into Free School Lane. This takes you past the **Whipple Museum.** Turn left after St. Benets Parish Church and turn right into King's Parade.

4. Stop at the gold plated **Corpus Clock,** with the grasshopper on top showing time being eaten

up. At odd times, the eyes blink. It is conceived and funded by John Taylor. He put one million pounds of his own  money into the project, which took 5 years. It also involved making explosions in a vacuum in a secret military unit in Holland to make the gold plated disc. The inscription is in Latin, and means *'The world passeth away, and the lust thereof'*.

5. If you want a shorter walk, carry on walking towards King's College and Great St.  Mary's Church. This is where you can climb the tower, very steep steps! There are relief maps of

Cambridge city outside. Carry along Trinity Street towards the Round Church.

6. OR - If little legs can take it, go for the longer walk by the backs. Cross the road to walk down the lane to Granta Place and the **Mill Pond.** This is a nice place to stop on a summers day, to have a picnic.

7. Walk over the bridge and across to Queens College. The next right is a path across a green that will take you on to **the backs of Kings and other colleges**. In the spring it is full of crocuses and daffodils.

8. The **Garrett Hostel Lane** takes you over a bridge with a lovely view of  Trinity Hall and Clare College. The cobbled street bends around into Trinity Lane past Gonville and Caius College.

9. Then you can either choose to walk into town for the shops, the market, or a cafe (Tatties is closest on Trinity Street).

10. Or you can go left past **Trinity College** and the tempting Old Sweet Shop. Over the road is

the medieval **Round Church**.

11. Look out in the pavement for the **brass flower studding.** 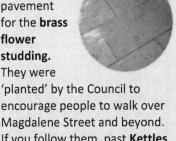 They were 'planted' by the Council to encourage people to walk over Magdalene Street and beyond. If you follow them, past **Kettles Yard Art Gallery** you'll see **Castle Hill,** on the right with views of all of Cambridge. It is a short steep climb.

PEOPLE OF CAMBRIDGE

People who lived or studied in Cambridge include:
Isaac Newton *(Trinity College)*
Charles Darwin *(Christ's College)*
Samuel Pepys *(Writer)*
John Major *(Prime Minister)*
Stephen Hawking *(Scientist)*
John Maynard Keynes *(Economist)*
Douglas Adams *(Writer)*
Keith Palmer of The Prodigy *(Musician)*
Richard Attenborough *(Actor)*
Snowy Farr *(Fundraiser)*
Francis Crick & James Watson *(DNA)*
Sir Francis Bacon - student aged 12 *(scientific method)*

SIR ISAAC NEWTON

He was an English physicist and mathematician and is most famous for discovering the laws of gravity. His Laws of Motion and Universal Gravitation laid the basis for much of modern science of the universe. He was a fellow of Trinity College, Cambridge.

He was bought up by his grandmother, never married, and was destined to become a farmer but he hated it. Partly out of revenge for a school bully, he became the top ranked student at his school, leading him to Cambridge University.

Newton said that he was partially inspired by watching the fall of an apple from a tree. Although there is no evidence it fell on his head. Reputed descendants of the tree are still at Trinity College

SNOWY FARR

I remember seeing Snowy when I was a child in Cambridge. He used to busk in the city centre and was unmistakable by his eccentric red military coat and top hat which often had white mice.

He was a colourful character, who raised thousands of pounds for The Guide Dogs of the Blind Association. He received an MBE for his efforts.

THE RIVER CAM

This slow moving river winds and curls its way around the meadows and colleges of Cambridge. It is like a green lung, preserving the open grasslands around it through the city centre and beyond.

Rowing on the Cam

From Midsummer Common northwards there are several rowing club houses on the west side of the river, and in the mornings you can often see the clubs practising for the various races. The 'May' bumps are in June, where crews aim to get a higher position by catching the boat ahead before getting 'bumped' from behind. The Oxford and Cambridge Boat Race takes place around Easter along the River Thames.

Punting along the River

This is the archetypal romantic view of Cambridge, with slowly gliding

punts moving past the historic colleges and past the weeping willows. In reality it does get quite busy in summer. Be aware that sometimes people do fall in. That said, it can be a fun day out, especially for visitors. Many of the punting companies provide life jackets for children on request. You may want to have a 'chauffeur' punt, if you have children. If you punt yourself, sometimes you can get stuck holding on to the pole in mud!

Cambridge Punt Company www.cambridgepuntcompany.co.uk
Cambridge Chauffer Punts www.punting-in-cambridge.co.uk
Granta www.puntingincambridge.com
Lets go Punting www.letsgopunting.co.uk
Scudamore's www.scudamores.com

Rainy Days

Arts Picture House which all have special children showings. There are toddler short films, reduced price Saturday films and baby/parent times. There are five local theatres.

If you fancy letting the kids run around and let off steam, there are soft play areas like the **Funky Fun House**, **Cheeky Monkeys Play Barn,** swimming pools and leisure centres.

It is raining outside but the little ones are getting restless. What is there to do?

There are some great museums in Cambridge, most of them free. My personal favourites are the **Fitzwilliam Museum** but there are many others.

There are three good local cinemas; **Cineworld**, **Vue** and the

There are some great indoor swimming pools and sports centres such as **Parkside Pool, Kelsey Kerridge** or **Chesterton** Sports Centre. This section lists all the local centres.

Alternatively, you can put on the raincoats, umbrellas and wellies, head out into rain and let the kids splash in puddles!

Theatres

ADC Theatre

This is the oldest University playhouse, behind the Round Church. The resident company is the Cambridge University Amateur Dramatic Club whose alumni include Sir Derek Jacobi and Stephen Fry.

Park Street, Cambridge CB5 8AS
Tel: 01223 300085
Boxoffice@adctheatre.com
www.adctheatre.com

Cambridge Arts Theatre

This is right in the heart of Cambridge, with regular national and local productions.

6 St. Edwards Passage,
Cambridge CB2 3PJ
Tel: 01223 503333
info@cambridgeartstheatre.com
www.cambridgeartstheatre.com

Corn Exchange Theatre

This is Cambridge's largest venue, it has regularly scheduled children's theatre and family events. It is an historic building, you can still see the farmers and plough on the front. It also has a cafe.

Wheeler Street, Cambridge CB2 3QB
Tel: 01223 357851
admin.cornex@cambridge.gov.uk
www.cornex.co.uk

The Junction

Off Hills Road near the Railway Bridge. This has a variety of cultural programmes, music, theatre and events, and a youth programme for teenagers. Regular theatre shows for families.

Clifton Way, Cambridge CB1 7GX
Tel: 01223 511511
tickets@junction.co.uk
www.junction.co.uk

The Mumford Theatre

This has a range of touring professional, local community and student theatre, as well as music events including free lunchtime concerts.

Anglia Ruskin University,
Cambridge, CB1 1PT
Tel: 01223 352932
mumford@anglia.ac.uk
www.anglia.ac.uk/mumfordtheatre

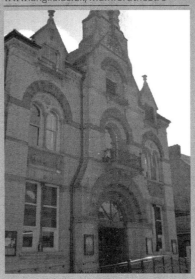

Museums and Galleries

All those listed below are FREE admission *except* the Cambridge Science Centre, Cambridge Museum of Technology and Centre for Computing History.

Cambridge and County Folk Museum

This interactive museum displays the everyday life of Cambridgeshire people. Originally the 'White Horse Inn', it contains art, costumes, textiles and toys from 1700 onwards. There are many interesting objects that tell of the past. See the blue glass 'Witch Balls', which were once hung in windows for protection; saintly statues from Hobson's Conduit; or a mangle for washing clothes.

2/3 Castle Street, Cambridge CB3 0AQ
Tel: 01223 355159
www.folkmuseum.org.uk
Open: Mon - Fri 10am-1pm, 2-5pm
FREE

Cambridge Museum of Technology

Sited by the River Cam, the Museum is housed in the Old Pumping Station. This was set up to pump

sewage into a sewage farm at Milton, and closed down in 1968. Originally the power came from steam. The city's rubbish was burned here to produce the steam, an early recycling unit! Families can borrow a mini toolbox of activities, see the big steam engines or dress up in Victorian clothes.

Cheddars Lane, Cambridge CB5 8LD
Tel: 01223 368650
www.museumoftechnology.com
Open: Easter–October every Sunday 2-5pm; November–Easter first Sunday of the month 2-5pm.
Admission: Non-steam days; Adults £3.50, children £1.50. Steam days; Adults £5.50, children £3.00

Cambridge Science Centre

The centre is a new venue for exhibitions, shows and workshops. It is a great place for kids to learn about science, particularly in a place like Cambridge where so many exciting research takes place all around us. It is a registered education charity There are regular science sessions such as 'Make a Bug, - learning about infectious disease; 'The secret world of the nano'; 'Extreme engineering' and more.

Learn about light thought mixing different combinations of colours, drop a magnet and generate electricity, see how the eye works feel and see sound, and see inside DNA.

18 Jesus Lane, Cambridge CB5 8BQ
Tel: 01223 967965
www.cambridgesciencecentre.org
Open: Tue–Fri 1-5pm (term time); weekends, half terms & holidays 10am–5pm.
Admission: Adults £3.50, child £2.50, under 5s free. Annual pass: family £25, adult £10, child £7

Cambridge University Museum of Archaeology and Anthropology

This has artefacts from all the world, founded in 1884. It is one of the most important collections in this area in the UK. The oldest object is a 1.8 million year old stone tool. It houses a large collection of objects from the voyages of Captain James Cook and Fiji. See the Iron Age 'Fire Dog', human skull made with shells, Egyptian hedgehog amulet and an X-ray of Ibis Mummy. Or a soul-washer's badge and model of a man smoking a pipe while carrying gunpowder from Ghana. There is a snakes and ladders board from India,

Samurai Armour from Japan and a Crocodile Mask from Torres Strait.

Downing St, Cambridge CB2 3DZ
Tel: 01223 333516
www.maa.cam.ac.uk
Open: Tue–Sat 10:30am–4:30pm; Sun 12 noon–4:30pm
Closed Mondays (except for bank holidays)
FREE

Centre for Computing History

A unique place, showing how computing has changed dramatically over the years. It is a bit out of the way, but if you have a computer interested child, or want to relive the old console games yourself, then it is worth the trek.

Rene Court, Coldhams Road, Cambridge CB1 3EW
Open: Weds to Sunday 10-5pm (last admission 4pm).
Admission: £7 Adults, £5 Children. Under 5s free.

Getting there: Close to the Beehive Centre in Cambridge.

Fitzwilliam Museum

A fantastic place to take the kids. The suits of armour, for horses and their knights, impressive staircase and artefacts from around the world really inspire the imagination. It was founded in 1848.

There are 30 galleries on two main levels. The ancient world is a favourite with my kids. See engraved fantastical animals in the Babylonian, Assyrian and Egyptian collections. It has the sarcophagus lid of Ramesses III from the Valley of the Kings.

It is one of the best museums on the country. Richard, VII Viscount Fitzwilliam of Merrion bequeathed the University of Cambridge his works of art and library in 1816 with funds to house them. There are now 20,000 pieces of decorative arts and sculpture from all over the world.

The marble staircase and grand entrance are very impressive. There is a shop, a good cafe and a lift to the different floors. The colour coded activity packs for kids are free from the entrance desks. They have interactive games and puzzles inside. There are also regular family drawing sessions (usually on the first Saturday of the month).

Trumpington St Cambridge CB2 1RB
Tel: 01223 332900
www.fitzmuseum.cam.ac.uk
Open: Tue–Fri 10am–5pm Sun & bank holiday Monday 12 noon–5pm.
Closed Mondays (except for bank holidays).
FREE

Kettle's Yard

CLOSED for redevelopment from June 2015. Due to reopen in 2017.

Kettle's Yard is a house with a permanent collection of 20th century art. It is the home of HS 'Jim' Ede, a former curator of the Tate Gallery in London. He described himself as an artists friend, and much of the art was acquired through his friendships. He devoted as much care in the display of the art, and how they interacted with each other and the space in the house, that this has been preserved now.

The gallery is a beautifully maintained home and much bigger on the inside. See his collections of Miró, Henry Moore, Alfred Wallis, Christopher Wood, David Jones, Ben and Winifred Nicholson and Henri Gaudier-Brzeska. However the house is like a word of art in itself. There are family events, such as drop in and draw sessions.

The new development will create an Education Wing, a cafe and environmentally controlled galleries.

Castle St Cambridge CB3 0AQ
Tel: 01223 748100
www.kettlesyard.co.uk
Open: House Tue–Sun 2–4pm , gallery Tue–Sun 11.30am–5pm
Closed Mondays (except for bank holidays)
FREE

Museum of Classical Archaeology

Explore the ancient classical civilisations. There are over 450 casts that cover the ancient world of Greece and Rome. These include a painted Peplos Kore. She is a type of statue, a model of a young woman to mark graves as an offering to the Gods.

We think of statues as white. However the Greeks liked to paint theirs in bright colours and adorn them with jewellery.

See the statues that would have at the Temple of Zeus in Olympia, the Farnese Hercules and more. Ask for alternative access if you have a buggy at thereception. They ask that kids are kept from touching the casts.

There are kids activities such an art material, trails, toddler boxes and even foam blocks to build a temple.

Faculty of Classics, Sidgwick Avenue, Cambridge CB3 9DA
Tel: 01223 330402
www.classics.cam.ac.uk/museum
Open: Mon–Fri 10am–5pm; Sat (term time only) 10am–1pm.
FREE

Museum of Zoology

CLOSED - due to reopen in 2016.

This is a great museum, with a huge Finback Whale skeleton and plenty to amuse the kids on a rainy day. It has close links with Darwin's work from the HMS Beagle bound for South America.

There are skeletons of a Killer Whale, Elephant, Giraffe. A collection of Darwin's beetles, and a giant crab. There is a young zoologists club for 6-13 year olds. It is free and members receive a welcome pack, a newsletter and priority booking for special events.

The Heritage Lottery Fund (HLF) has awarded a grant of £1.8 million, which will go towards refurbishment. There will be a new Whale Hall two storey's high, and a brand new updated space for the collection.

Downing St, Cambridge CB2 3EJ
Tel: 01223 336650
www.museum.zoo.cam.ac.uk
FREE

Sedgewick Museum of Earth Sciences

Look out for the dinosaurs carved above the door, and the world's biggest spider inside. This is the oldest of the University museums, established in 1728. There are over 2 million fossils, minerals and rocks from 4.5 billion years ago.

Spot the bronze statue of Adam Sedgwick inside. He holds his geological hammer in one hand, and in another, a fossil. If you look at it you will see it contains a trilobite,

which is half a billion years old. The huge Iguanodon dinosaur skeleton guards the entrance. The discovery of this creature was vital to understanding more about dinosaurs. There is also a giant deer and a hippopotamus from Cambridgeshire.

Downing St, Cambridge CB2 3EQ
Tel: 01223 333456
www.sedgwickmuseum.org
Open: Mon - Fri 10:00-13:00, 14:00 17:00 Sat 10:00-16:00
FREE

The Polar Museum

The Institute was established in 1920 by Frank Debenham as a memorial to Scott and his companions. It holds a unique collection of paintings, photographs, maps, equipment and journals from the Arctic and Antarctic.

It has exhibitions of Sir Ernest Shackleton and his Trans-Antarctic Endurance Expedition in 1914. It also houses artefacts from Captain Scott. There are hunting spears and bows from native Eskimo.

You can see decorated teeth and tusks from Walrus and Whale bone. These were made by sailors, who spent hours toiling away on long whaling voyages in the 1800s.

Lensfield Road, Cambridge CB2 1EP
Tel: 01223 336540   www.spri.cam.ac.uk
Open: Tue - Fri 10:00-16:00   *CLOSED: Sundays, Mondays and bank holiday Saturdays. Open on bank holiday Mondays. Groups (max 25) should book in advance.*
FREE

Whipple museum of the History of Science

This holds a pre-eminent collection of scientific instruments and models, dating from the Middle Ages to the present. It was founded in 1944 by Robert Stewart Whipple, who donated his collection of scientific instruments to the University.

You can see the large telescopes used in the 18th century, see how people navigated around the glove, the old sundials and mathematical instruments. There are some fascinating objects, such a silver celestial planisphere. This shows the stars in the sky, along with engraved pictures and degrees. The armillary spheres are models of the universe.

The collection includes many of the instruments used in the Cav-

endish Laboratory. This includes an X Ray tube, Electrical instruments used to make amazing discoveries through the last centuries.

Free School Lane, Cambridge CB2 3RH
Tel: 01223 330906
www.hps.cam.ac.uk/whipple
Open: Mon - Fri 12.30-16:30
CLOSED: Bank holidays
FREE

Wysing Arts Centre

This is a place for artistic experimentation and discovery, with exhibitions and events. It is on a large rural site outside Cambridge city, in a 17th century farmhouse, in the village of Bourn. It doesn't have a cafe, but there are nearby places to eat.

Fox Road, Bourn, Cambridge CB23 2TX
Tel: 01954 718881
www.wysingartscentre.org
Open: Daily 12 noon–5pm when there is an exhibition in the gallery. Check the website to be sure. *CLOSED:* Bank Holiday Mondays and when there are no exhibitions.

Other Places of Historic Interest in Cambridge

Cherry Hinton Hall

A Victorian country house set in a beautiful (now public) park, built by John Oakes, who used to be a surgeon at Addenbrooke's Hospital. The grounds are well known for hosting the annual Cambridge Folk Festival. Great childrens play area, paddling pool, large ponds and grass spaces.

The island in the pool is known locally as Giants Grave, after the giant Gogmagog. Or it may also have come from some Iron Age burials which were excavated on Lime Kiln Hill, where the skeletons were unusually tall (found in 1854). It is also the site of a spring which provided a major water supply to Cambridge in 19th century. The Hall itself is now owned by Cambridge City Council. It

was built in 1839 in Elizabethan style, and includes a Butler's Pantry and spiral staircase.

Cherry Hinton Road, Cambridge, CB1 8DB

The Leper Chapel

Cambridge's oldest complete building, the Chapel of St Mary Magdalene, also known as the Leper Chapel dates back to the 12th century. It was built as part of an isolation hospital for lepers. In 1199 King John granted the Hospital the right to hold a three-day fair on the Vigil of Holy Cross.

Rent from the stalls boosted the income, and it grew into Stourbridge Fair, the largest medieval fair in Europe which lasted until 1933. Goods included silk, wool, garlic, cheese and hops, reflected now in the names of the nearby streets (Garlic Row,Oyster Row, Cheddars Lane). Every September the fair is recreated in a smaller way, with medieval dancing, history talks, peddlars, an alchemist and stalls selling similar goods. There is even a University of Cambridge Proctor and Constables to police the event!

Barnwell Junction on the Newmarket Road, Cambridge, CB5 8JJ
(opposite Cambridge United Football Ground)

Getting there: Bus - Citi 3 and get off at Coldhams common/Ditton Walk stop.

Library Rhyme & Stories

There are free rhymetimes and story times in most local libraries.

Cambridge Central Library

1st Floor, 7 Lion Yd,
Cambridge CB2 3QD
Tel: 0345 045 5225

Free '**Rhymetime**' from birth - 18 months.
Tuesday at 2:30-3pm
Thursday at 2:30-3pm & 3:15 3:45pm
Friday at at 2:30-3pm
Saturday at 10:30-11am

Storytime for children from 18 months to 5 years
Mondays 10:30-11am
Sunday 3-3:30pm

This has a good children's section, for younger and older children and teenagers. In the summer, children can take part in the Summer Reading Challenge.

You could be eligible for the Bookstart Bear Club (free membership, baby and treasure pack), often from your health visitor in the first year of your child's life.

Local Libraries

Most local libraries have a toddler session, see times at:
https://cambridgewithkids.com/library-storytime1/

Cinemas

Arts Picture House Cinema

This 3 screen arts cinema shows a wide variety of films. There is a Kid's Club on Saturdays suitable for 3–10 year olds. On Wednesday morning is Big Scream, a club for new parents and their babies (under 1 year). Toddler time is 30 minute shows for pre-school children. Autism friendly screenings have low lights and volume.

38-39 St Andrew's St, Cambridge CB2 3AR
Tel: 0871 902 5720

The Light Cinema (formerly Cineworld)

Multi 9 screen cinema complex at Cambridge Leisure Park. Places to eat nearby. Has movies for juniors, at a cheap rate on Saturday, autism friendly screenings.

Cambridge Leisure Park, Clifton Way, Cambridge CB1 7DY
Tel: 01223 612210

Vue Cinema

Eight screen cinema within the Grafton Centre. Kids AM club screens a selected kids film every Saturday and Sunday and every day in school holidays for a cheap rate. Also teen tickets, up to 20% off adult price.

The Grafton Centre, East Rd, Cambridge CB1 1PS
Tel: 0871 224 0240

Soft Play Centres

Cheeky Monkeys Activity Centre

A farm based playbarn in Fulbourn, 4 miles east of Cambridge. It has plenty of space for kids to let off steam. It has an outdoor play tractors, playhouse, sandpit and indoor soft play. There is a cafe too, and in the summer strawberry and raspberry picking.

Babraham Rd Fulbourn CB21 5HR
Tel: 01223 881658
Admission: £3.80/4.50 per child
Open: Term time Tue to Sun 10-5pm (closed Mondays).

Funky Fun House

Indoor family play centre. Soft play, slides, a sports pitch, special play areas for babies and for toddlers, party rooms and an on-site cafe make this good for rainy days.

8 Mercers Row Cambridge CB5 8HY
Tel: 01223 304705
Admission: £3.70/4.50 per child.
Open: Every day in school holidays 10-6pm. Term time closed Tues & Thurs

Whale of a Time

Play areas for Crawlers and Toddlers and older soft play and multi adventure.

8 Viking Way, Bar Hill, CB3 8EL
Tel: 01954 781018
Admission: £4/4.50 per child
Open: Every day 10-5pm

Swimming & Sports

Indoor Swims

Abbey Swimming Pool

Swimming lessons, aqua aerobics. It also has an exercise studio, Astro-turf pitch, grass pitch, fitness suite.

Whitehill Road, Cambridge CB5 8NT
Tel: 01223 213352

Chesterton Sports Centre

This has a swimming pool, as well as sports facilities. Children's swimming lessons including Rookie Lifeguard and Synchronised Swimming.

Gilbert Road, Cambridge CB4 3NY
Tel: 01223 576 110

King's Hedges Learner Swimming Pool

This is a 15m pool. It runs swimming lessons for children from 5 months upwards.

Jedburgh Court, Buchan St, Cambridge CB4 2XH
Tel: 01223 353248

Parkside Swimming Pool

Parkside Pool is the biggest in Cambridge with eight lanes, 25 m long competition standard. It has a children's pool and two flume rides. It is sometimes closed to the public for competitions.

Gonville Place, Cambridge CB1 1LY
Tel: 01223 446100

Outdoor Swims

All the listed outdoor paddling pools are free to use, except Jesus Green. Open May to September.

Cherry Hinton Water Play Area

These two small paddling pools are in the grounds of Cherry Hinton Hall. The water shelves gently to a maximum depth of 0.4 metres, and the pools are fenced in for safety.

Cherry Hinton Hall, Cherry Hinton Rd, Cambridge CB1 8DW
Tel: 01223 213352

Coleridge Paddling Pool

The pool is fenced off, with seating and toilets available nearby. The pool varies from 0.2 to 0.45 metres in depth.

Coleridge recreation ground, Davy Rd, Cambridge
Tel: 01223 213352

Jesus Green Outdoor Lido

Usually Monday to Sunday 10:30 to 7:30pm, earlier on Tuesday and Friday. Great outdoor pool on Jesus Green, perfect for a sunny day. There is an admission charge.

Jesus Green, Off Chesterton Rd, Cambridge CB4 3AX

Tel: 01223 302579

Sheeps Green Learner Pool

The pool is 0.9 metres deep and is free to use. Male and female changing rooms are available. A lifeguard is present during opening hours, which are 10am-5.30pm, Monday to Sunday. The site also has a large playground, toilets and a refreshment kiosk.

Lammas Land / Sheep's Green via Barton Road, Cambridge
Tel: 01223 302580

Sports Centres

Cambourne Sports Centre

Four court sports hall, exercise studio, fitness suite.

Back Lane, Great Cambourne CB23 6FY
Tel: 01954 714070

Chesterton Sports Centre (see also previous page)

17 metre swimming pool for training or fun. Sports hall, tennis courts, astroturf, gym and cafe.

Gilbert Road, Cambridge CB4 3NY
Tel: 01223 576 110

Kelsey Kerridge

It is the largest sports hall in the Cambridge area. Activities include badminton, football, basketball and volleyball. There is a long mirrored room with a sports floor for archery, table tennis, martial arts, cricket, and fitness studio. Outlooks gym and free weights gym.

Queen Anne Terrace, Cambridge CB1 1NA
Tel: 01223 462226

Netherhall Sports Centre

Sports hall, gym, dance studio, atrium hall, football pitch, 5 floodlit netball/tennis courts, grass pitches.

Queen Edith's Way, Cambridge CB1 8NN
Tel: 01223 712142

The Park - Cambridge Regional College Sports

There are two squash courts, two sports halls, climbing wall, Gym, exercise studio, floodlit outdoor 5-a-side all weather pitch. Varied activities.

Kings Hedges Road, Cambridge CB4 2QT
Tel: 01223 418280

Eating Out

There are some great places to eat in Cambridge, from breakfast cafes to upmarket restaurants. I have found these to be reliable and welcoming of children, however there are many more.

Bella Italia (Italian)

Good value children's menu, three courses and drink for £5.45, with an activity book. There are also two other restaurants in the Grafton Centre and Cambridge Leisure Park.

The Watermill, Newnham Road, Cambridge CB3 9EY
Tel: 01223 367507
Open: Mon - Thu: 09:00-23:00
Fri - Sat: 09:00 - 00:00 Sun: 09:00 - 22:30

Browns (Classic)

This is a large restaurant directly opposite the Fitzwilliam Museum, and serves classic food. It has a more adventurous children's menu than most, including crab & tiger prawn linguine as well as burgers.

23 Trumpington Street, Cambridge CB2 1QA
Tel: 01223 461655   **Open:** Mon-Thu: 09:30-23:00, Fri & Sat 12:00 23:00, Sun 12:00-22:30

Byron Burgers

Described as 'proper' burgers, using Scottish beef. It has a simple but tasty kids menu, with macaroni cheese and mini burgers.

12 Bridge Street, Cambridge CB2 1UF
Tel: 01223 462927
Open: Mon-Sat 11.00-23.00. Sun 11.00-22.30

Charlie Chan (Chinese)

This is one of the oldest restaurants in Cambridge. It used to be called the Pagoda and is a family run place. Downstairs is more casual, for family dinners or lunches.

14 Regent St Cambridge CB2 1DB
Tel: 01223 359336
Open: Mon - Sat: 11:30am-10.30pm

Clowns (Italian)

This is a great laid back, warm, family run place, and has good reasonably priced Italian dishes. The pasta dishes are great. It is decorated with paintings of clowns.

54 Kings Street, Cambridge CB1 1LN
Tel: 01223 355711
Open: Mon-Sun: 8:00-23:00

Frankie & Benny's (Italian)

It has a varied kids and juniors menu and organic baby food. All the main kid staples are catered for like spaghetti bolognaise, bananas and custard, burgers and ice-cream.

Cambridge Leisure Park, Clifton Way, Cambridge CB1 7DY
Tel: 01223 412430
Open: Mon - Sat:: 09:00-23:00, Sun: 09:00-22.30

Lalbagh Bangladeshi & Indian Diner

A very good eat in and take away, not central but nice food. It doesn't have a children's menu.

49 Alms Hill Bourn, Cambridge CB23 2SH
Tel: 01954 719131   **Open:**
Mon to Sun 12:00-14:00, 17:30-22:30

Livingstones Cafe

Cafe in the church with an area for kids to play. A quiet retreat from the busy centre.

St Andrew's Baptist Church, St Andrew's St, Cambridge www.stasbaptist.org
Open: 10-4pm Mon - Sat

Marks & Spencer Cafe

Upstairs at the store. This has a good children's meal deal that includes fruit, a drink and a snack.

5 Market Hill, Cambridge CB2 3NJ
Tel: 01223 355219

Pizza Express

It doesn't have the pizza express sign on the outside, as it is located in the historic Pitt club building near Jesus College. It has a 'piccolo' children's menu, with activity pack. Try the

Banbinoccino (a little cappuccino without the coffee).

7a Jesus Lane, Cambridge CB5 8BA
Tel: 01223 324033
Open: Mon-Sun 11.30-23:00

Pizza Hut

The kids menu includes an all you can eat salad, and it has an ice cream factory. There is also a restaurant at Newmarket Road and Cambridge Leisure Park.

19-21 Regent Street, Cambridge CB2 1AB
Tel: 01223 323737
Open: Sun-Thu: 12:00-22:00 Fri-Sat: 11:00-23:00

Rainbow Cafe (Vegetarian)

This popular cafe has been serving vegetarian food for 20 years. Tasty soups and cakes and healthy main dishes. They provide free organic baby food and a children's menu of pasta or half meals.

9a King's Parade, Cambridge CB2 1SJ
Tel: 01223 902138
Open: Sun: 10:00-16:00, Mon: Closed. Tue - Sat: 10:00-22:00

Sticky Beaks (Home Baking)

Lovely cakes, like butterscotch layer cake. Lunch salads include chickpea, butternut squash and feta cheese. In the town centre.

42 Hobson St, Cambridge CB1 3NL
Tel: 01223 359397
Open: Mon-Fri 08:00-17:30, Sat 09:00-17:30 Sun 10:00-17:00

Tatties (Cafe)

This is a budget choice, and great for hungry kids if you are shopping in town. It gets very busy, but service is fast.

11 Sussex Street, Cambridge CB2 1TB
Tel: 01223 323399 **Open:**
Mon-Sat: 08:30-19:00, Sun: 10:00-17:00

The Blue Lion (Pub Fare)

Good classic cooking, using locally sourced ingredients. It does a children's menu and gluten free menu.

74 Main Street, Hardwick CB23 7QU
Tel: 01954 210328
Open: Mon to Fri: 12:00-14:30, 18:00
21:00 Sat: 12:00-21:00, Sun: 12:00-20:00

The Orchard Tea Gardens

This historic place sells lovely scones and tea, and on a summer's day you can sit on one of the deckchairs in the orchard. It is a welcome treat after a walk to Grantchester. Poets like Byron used to come here.

45-47 Mill Way, Grantchester, Cambridge
CB3 9ND
Tel: 01223 845788
Open: Mon-Sun: 10:00-16:00

The Sea Tree

Really good fish bar. It has an eat-in and take-away menu. Kids can have handmade fishfingers and chips.

13-14 The Broadway, Mill Rd, Cambridge CB1 3AH
Tel: 01223 414349
Open: Mon 17:00-22:00, Tue to Fri 12:00-14:00, 17:00-22:00, Sat 12:00-22:00. Sun 17:00-21:00

Urban Larder

Good locally sourced food, such as local honey, cheeses from the Wobbly Botttom Farm and jams from the W.I. Ladies. Known for its pies, pasties and baked goods.

No. 9 The Broadway, Mill Rd, Cambridge CB1 3AH
Tel: 01223 212462
Open: 8-6pm

Yippee Noodle Bar

Fresh and fast noodles in this informal and tasty bar. You can find it right in the heart of the city.

7-9 King Street, Cambridge, CB1 1LH
Tel: 01223 518111
www.yippeenoodlebar.co.uk
Open: Sat & Sun: 12 - 10pm; Mon - Fri: 12 - 3pm & 5pm - 10pm

Zhonghua Traditional Snacks

This is a small, cosy restaurant serving Chinese handmade dumplings and noodle dishes. Reasonable prices and good service.

13 Norfolk Street, Cambridge CB1 2LD
Tel: 01223 354573
Open: Mon, Wed - Sun 12-9pm. Closed Tuesdays.

Bump to Baby

From thinking about wanting to have a baby, to becoming pregnant and being a first time parent can be quite a journey. Your GP or information from the NHS is the first contact if you are trying to conceive or are pregnant. In addition, in Cambridge there are a huge range of antenatal classes and support.

Maternity Care

When you first suspect that you are pregnant, visit your local health centre or GP who will then be able to explain your maternity or 'antenatal' care. You will be offered appointments to check your progress. You will also be offered antenatal classes and breastfeeding workshops. All hospitals offer at least two ultrasound scans during pregnancy, the first around 8-14 weeks, or 'dating scan', and the second between 18 and 21 weeks.

NHS Choices

NHS Choices has a wealth of information on pregnancy, maternity services, the birth and early years.

www.nhs.uk/Conditions/pregnancy-and-baby

National Childbirth Trust (NCT)

This has a local branch run by volunteers and offers support for parents and those who are pregnant. It can be a good way of getting to know local parents.

Tel: 0844 243 6896
Chair@NCTCambridge.org
Antenatal and postnatal classes:
bookings5g@nct.org.uk or

Adoption & Fostering

You can obtain an information pack from Cambridgeshire County Council, which has comprehensive information if you are considering fostering or adopting a child.

Cambridgeshire County Council
Tel; 0800 052 0078
www.cambridgeshire.gov.uk/childrenandfamilies/parenting

Rosie Hospital

The Rosie Hospital at Addenbrooke's is the main maternity service in Cambridge. You can usually choose to have your baby in a hospital, a midwife-led unit or at home, depending on your health and your pregnancy.

Rosie Hospital, Robinson Way
Cambridge CB2 0QQ
Tel: 01223 217 617
www.cuh.org.uk/cms/rosie-hospital

Antenatal & Postnatal Classes

There are many in Cambridge; hypnotherapy for birth, yoga, baby signing, rhymes and music. Check the website for more up to date details of classes.
www.cambridgewithkids.com

Time Out

Not for kids, for parents/carers! Being a carer of children, particularly young children, can be a demanding job. It can be hard to take time off to take care of yourself.

If you are able to get some time off, there are many places in and outside of Cambridge to relax and indulge, such as a spa treatment at 'The Park' at Cambridge Regional College, which offers affordable rates. If you want to keep in shape, there are gyms with an attached crèche.

If you are missing the cinema and have a baby, there are special 'Big Scream' screenings at the Arts Picture House. Longer term, you may be considering your career, re-training or volunteering. If you are a single parent, it can be even harder to get time off, however there are support groups (p 127).

Pampering & Relaxation

The Varsity Hotel & Spa
Thompson's Lane (off Bridge street), Cambridge CB5 8AQ
Tel: +44 (0)1223 30 60 30 l
info@thevarsityhotel.co.uk
www.thevarsityhotel.co.uk

Elemis Spa
The Glassworks Gym
Thompson's Lane (Off Bridge Street), Cambridge CB5 8AQ
Tel: 01223 305060
contact@theglassworksgym.co.uk

Imagine Spa
Best Western Cambridge Quy Mill Hotel, Church Road, Stow-Cum-Quy, Cambridge CB25 9AF
Tel: 01223 294179
imaginespa.co.uk/quymill
quymill@imaginespa.co.uk

Lxir Spa Caruso
70 Regent St, Cambridge
Tel: 01223 300777
www.lxirspacaruso.co.uk

The Park
Beauty Salon and Hairdresser
Cambridge Regional College, Kings Hedges Road, Cambridge CB4 2QT
Tel: 01223 418998
Affordable prices and hairdressing. Different rates if service by students.

Babysitters

It is not easy to find someone that you trust to mind your child If you decide to get a babysitter, whether a friend, family or professional service, consider their experience, whether they have first aid training, how they will play, deal with a tantrum or problem with your child. Ask for references and follow these up. You will need to decide if they are responsible enough to look after your child and handle an emergency. The NSPCC www.nspcc.org.uk/help-and-advice/for-parents/keeping-your-child-safe

Ofsted
www.ofsted.gov.uk
For a list of registered childminders.

Gyms With Crèche's

David Lloyd
Coldham's Business Park Coldham's Lane Cambridge CB1 3LH
www.davidlloyd.co.uk/home/families
Children's gym. Soft play area.

Spirit Health Club Cambridge
Holiday Inn Cambridge, Lakeview, Bridge Road, Impington, Cambridge CB24 9PH
Tel: 01223 236620
spirit.cambridge@ihg.com
www.spirithealthclubs.co.uk/clubs
Beauty Treatments, Children's Play Area, Crèche on Mon, Tue and Fri mornings.

Movies

Staying in is the new going out! Well, it can be, if you have young children and limited or zero babysitting. However there are DVD rentals, box sets and satellite TV on demand features so that you can still see the latest movies at home. There is also the 'Big Scream', where you can watch a movie in a cinema if you are a parent with a baby under one.

Arts Picture House Cambridge - Big Scream
www.picturehouses.co.uk/cinema/Arts_Picturehouse_Cambridge/Whats_On/Clubs_Groups/Big_Scream/
Low lights are left on and nappy changing facilities for these movies exclusively for parents with babies under one year old. Usually on Wednesday mornings but check website. See page 48.

DVD Rentals & Satellite Options
There are so many options, and special offers these days. Check out www.moneysavingexpert.com for the best deals.

Education and Training

Cambridge Awise
info@camawise.org.uk
camawise.org.uk
The aim is to advance the participation of girls and women in the sciences.

Cambridge Central Library
7 Lion Yard, Grand Arcade, Cambridge CB2 3QD
Tel: 0345 045 5225
www.cambridgeshire.gov.uk/leisure
Access to public computers free to library members, photocopiers and printers. It is also linked to the National Adult Careers Service. The

learning centre gives free advice to help with deciding on the right training and employment for you. It is located at the top floor and runs an appointment system. Phone 01223 728512 to enquire.

Cambridge Women's Resource Center

CWRC The Wharf, Hooper Street, Cambridge CB1 2NZ
Tel: 01223 321148
www.cwrc.org.uk
A guidance worker is available to support women who want to move on into employment, training or education. There is also support with CVs and application forms. It has a creche during the day, Monday to Friday term time only (to be booked in advance). Training is available in English, Maths and other subjects. Many of these courses are free or very low rates.

National Careers Service

nationalcareersservice.direct.gov.uk
Provides advice and support on careers.

Open University

www.open.ac.uk
Distance learning, with flexible options which can fit around children.

Adult Careers Service Cambridgeshire

www.cambridgeshire.gov.uk/jobs
Tel: 07717 677940
Adult careers advisors for people in Cambridgeshire and Peterborough. It is also a useful search engine for local jobs.

Cambridge Evening News Jobs

www.cambridge.jobsnow.co.uk
Jobs in Cambridgeshire.

Centre 33 Young Carers Project

Tel: 01223 307488
youngcarers@centre33.org.uk
www.centre33.org.uk
The Project supports 8 - 18 year old young carers in and around Cambridge who support a family member with a long-term illness, disability, mental health problem or who misuse drugs or alcohol. They also look for volunteers with the centre.

Volunteering

Volunteer Centres Cambridgeshire
www.volunteeringcambsandpboro.org.uk
Tel: 01223 356549
www.cam-volunteer.org.uk
Helps to match people who want to volunteer with organisations needing volunteers. Everything from working with animals to helping out charities.

Home-Start

This voluntary scheme offers friendship, support and practical help to families with children under five years old. Particularly those families struggling to cope. Available in certain areas around Cambridgeshire.

Cambridge & District

The Fields Children's Centre, Galfrid Road, Cambridge CB5 8ND.
Tel: 01223 210202 or email:
office@homestartcambridge.co.uk

Travelling with Kids

It can help to think ahead when it comes to travelling with children. A baby needs a lot of equipment, a buggy and if bottle fed, formula and bottles. Toddler routines may get upset and teenagers may get bored. But do not be disheartened! It is possible to have a lot of fun with a bit of patience and practical help.

Travel Light - This may seem impossible, but it can really help not to have to lug a lot of bags. Check if hotels have travel cots ahead.

Toys/Games - If possible, try to bring only those that will really get a lot of use. Although pack an extra surprise book or toy in case. Kids can have their own bag.

Pack for Delays - Include extra nappies, snacks, change of clothes, colouring book, Ipad. Whatever keeps your child happy when bored.

Flying - Be prepared with liquids in a separate clear bag. Baby food/formula is allowed. Take a good, collapsible buggy.

Be Realistic - Allow for the fact that you have kids and don't expect too much out of yourself or them. Keep calm (if possible) and take care of your own stress levels. Sometimes it is the simplest things about travelling that are the best, so enjoy!

Families from Abroad

Whether you are coming for a job contract, or have moved to Cambridgeshire permanently, it can be a challenge to adjust to a new environment, and help children to settle in. Children may take a bit of time to settle into a new school.

It may help to get involved in activities in the school if you can, and arrange play dates to help your child socialise. You may want help learning English for you and/or your child. There are several English language teachers in Cambridge.

English as an Additional Language
Schools will usually be supportive, and you can help your child learn English at home. Cambridgeshire **Race and Equality Diversity Services (**CREDS) can support you if you need more help or advice.
Tel: 01223 703882

School Admissions

All children must legally start school in the term following their 5th birthday, although places are offered following your child's 4th birthday.

Admissions Team
CC1206, Castle Court, Castle Hill, Cambridge CB3 0AP
Tel 0345 045 1370
www.cambridgeshire.gov.uk/childrenandfamilies/education

Shopping

Grafton Shopping Centre

Between Newmarket Rd and
East Rd, Cambridge, CB1 1PS
Tel: 01223 316201

Late night shopping every
Wednesday. It has Mothercare, several fashion and phone shops, Debenhams, Boots, cafes, Burger King
and also houses Vue Cinema. Outside there are several charity shops in
Burleigh Street. They have a kid's
club, running craft activities once a
month.

Grand Arcade

St Andrew's St Cambridge, CB2 3BJ
Tel: 01223 302601

The newest indoor shopping area in
Cambridge, also open late night
shopping every Wednesday. It houses John Lewis, and several more up-market clothing, shoe, jewellery and
beauty stores. It joins on to Lions
Yard Shopping Centre.

Lions Yard Shopping Centre

St. Tibbs Row, Cambridge CB2 3ET
Tel: 01223 350608

The first shopping centre built in
Cambridge.

Mill Road

This is the place to go to find a great
variety of independent shops and
cafes. There are health food shops,
restaurants, take aways and cafes
plus late night convenience stores.

Includes the Sally Ann, the second
hand store.

Cambridge Market

Market Square, Cambridge

This is open seven days a week
and is still held in the ancient
square where it has been selling
fruit, vegetables and wares for
hundreds of years. It is right in the
middle of town in, of course, Market Square.

All Saints Garden Arts & Craft Market

All Saints Garden, Trinity St, Cambridge

Usually held on Saturdays, for local stalls selling art and crafts.

Cambridge City Centre

There is an impressive amount and
variety of shops in a compact and
mostly traffic free centre. Rose
Crescent, Trinity Street and Green
Street have some lovely boutique
stores. There is a Marks and Spencer (Market Square) and Sainsburies (Sidney Street) for food.

Public Toilets / Baby Changing

Chesterton Road
Drummer Street Bus Station
Gonville Place, Parker's Piece
Grafton Centre,   Jesus Green
Lammas Land,   Lion Yard
Park St Car Park
Quayside & Silver St
Victoria Avenue

10 Children's Party Ideas

1. **Kelsey Kerridge Sports Parties** Archery/football/basketball/trampolining and more. *www.kelseykerridge.co.uk*

2. **Sublime Science** – Provides potions, bubbles and magic tricks *www.sublimescience.com/kids-party-cambridge-entertainer*

3. **David Lloyd Pool Party** or Birthday party *www.davidlloyd.co.uk/home/families*

4. **Chesterton Sports Centre** -Birthday pool or Bouncy Fun party *www.chestertonsportscentre.org.uk/activities/birthday-parties*

5. **Si5 Spymissions,** which includes a meal and a secret spy mission. www.*spymissions.co.uk/parties*

6. **Craft Monkey Paint Your Own Pottery, Build a Bear,** St Neots. Can come to your venue. *www.craftymonkeypotterypainting.com*

7. **Pizza Express** – Make Your Own Pizza Party – with a balloon and certificate to take home. *www.pizzaexpress.com/parties/kidspizzamaking*

8. **Nature Activity Party at Wandlebury** – Based in the Stable Rooms, can be a nature discovery or twilight walk. Bring food, they have plates and beakers. www.*cambridgeppf.org/wandlebury-country-park*

9. **Carluccio's Picnic Punting Party** – Includes Italian Kids Picnic, punting and life vests. *www.puntingincambridge.com/Carluccios-kids*

10. **Cambridge Kung Fu Kids Party** – An hour of activity and Kung Fu moves with a mini ceremony where everyone gets a certificate. *www.cambridgekungfu.com/kids/parties*

Do It Yourself
Alternatively, you can organise your own party, with finger food, treats, fun and games, at your home or outside as a picnic. Smaller children could play traditional games like musical chairs or 'Simon says', and you can rope in help from other parents.

Some people hire a local hall or a bouncy castle. Party bags, if you want them, can work out expensive. Instead you could buy a set of books like the Mr Men series or do a lucky dip, or get the kids to decorate their own cup cake to take away.

Cycling

Cambridge is a fantastic place to cycle around. It is flat, relatively small and there are several cycle ways and off-road cycling paths. It has the highest levels of cycling in the UK. Cycling with children can be great fun. Cycle shops in the city can give advice on what to buy, safety and practicalities. There are local courses for kids on cycle safety.

Cycle Hire (& Purchase)

Bicycle Ambulance
Park Street, CB5 8AS
Tel: 07838 162572
bicycleambulance.com

City Cycle Hire
61 Newnham Road, CB3 9EY
Tel: 01223 365629
www.citycyclehire.com

Cambridge Station Cycles
7 Station Rd, CB1 2TZ
Tel: 01223 307125
Railstation@stationcycles.co.uk

Cambridge Station Cycles
Grand Arcade Cycle Park,
Corn Exchange St
Tel: 01223 307655

Cambridge City Council Pushchair Scheme

This is such a handy idea for parents who want to cycle into town but then need to push a young child around in a buggy. You can borrow a pushchair for free from the two covered cycle parks (see below) at **Station Cycles** and the **Bicycle Ambulance** shop.

Cycle Parks in Cambridge

There are two covered parks in the city (as well as many outdoor rails).
Park St car park - space for 200 cycles in basement. Cycle lockers available at £10 per month. Tel: 01223 458515. Bicycle Ambulance Shop.
Grand Arcade car park - space for 200 cycles. Closes 23:30. The Shop run by Station cycles has luggage lockers available at £2 per day.

Cycle Tours

Cambridge Bike Tours
Tel: 01223 366868
Info@cambridgebiketours.co.uk
www.cambridgebiketours.co.uk
Choice of tours, and can combine lunch, bikes and punting.

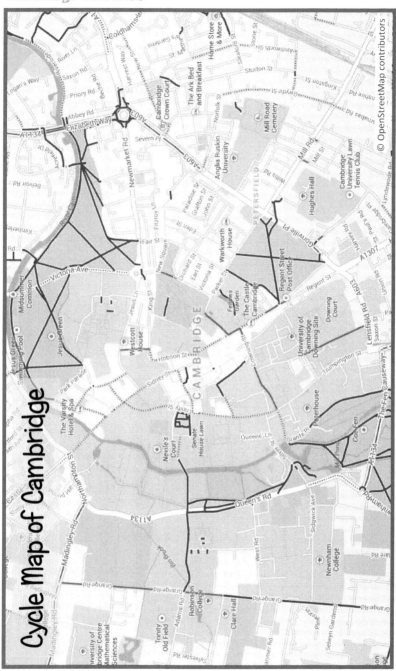

Cycle Map of Cambridge

Free stuff

There is much to do in Cambridge for free. Of course there are the parks and playgrounds. There are also free events, fantastic museums and story telling in libraries.

Free Events (p124)

*Cambridge Science Festival - **Mar***
*Ely Eel Day - **Apr***
*Arbury Carnival - **Jun***
*Strawberry Fair - Cambridge - **Jun***
*Cherry Hinton Festival - **Sep***
*Open Cambridge Weekend - **Sep***
*Cambridge Dragon Boat Festival - **Sep***
*Cambridge Festival of Ideas - **Oct***
*Bonfire Night - 5th **Nov***
*Milll Road Winter Fair - Cambridge -**Dec***

Museums (p40)

Cambridge and County Folk Museum
Cambridge Museum of Technology
Cambridge University Museum of Archaeology and Anthropology
Fitzwilliam Museum
Kettle's Yard
Scott Polar Research Institute
Sedgewick Museum of Earth Sciences
University Museum of Zoology

Whipple Museum of the History of Science

Library Stories (p47)

Various Libraries in Cambridgeshire.
Cambridge Central Library

Swimming (p49)

Some free sessions in indoor pools at certain times with a membership card.
Outdoor pools open in the summer, the following are free.

Lammas Land Outdoor Pool
Cherry Hinton Outdoor Pool

Wildlife & Country Parks

Some of these have a charge to go into the houses, but the grounds or parks are usually free.(p105)

Cherry Hinton Hall Grounds
Clare Castle Country Park
Grafham Water
Gog Magog Hills
Hinchingbrooke Country Park
Milton Country Park
Wandlebury Country Park and the Wimpole Estate Grounds
Walpole Water Gardens

ꝕꝓ Walks with Kids

Cambridge has a variety of walks that suit children, because it has so many open green spaces around the centre. If you have visitors who want to look around the colleges, then there are very short walks around the river and in the ancient and historic buildings, with the added bonus of being near cafes, public transport and shops if you need them.

To make walks more interesting, children of all ages can be inspired by a bit of knowledge about an areas social and geological history. For example did you know there is an ancient water course running underneath Jesus Green? Or that Castle Hill was where the earliest Cambridge people lived? Walk to see nature, like the autumn leaves, ducks or even bats.

And there are also some fantastic ways to make a mini detective out of your kids, with treasure walks or 'geocaching'. These are a fun way to make an adventure out of exploring.

TOP 10 WALKS

1 **Stourbridge Common to Fen Ditton**. A nice flat walk along the river. most of it suitable for buggies.

2 **River Walk to Grantchester.** End up in the Orchard Tea Room. eating a scone underneath the apples trees in a deck chair.

3 **Anglesey Abbey Walk**. Explore the fens around the Abbey. past Lode Mill

4 **Art Walk around Cambridge.** A tour around some of the sculptures, colleges and art in the city.

5 **Animals, Romans, Ancient Rivers.** Liven up a walk with some intriguing facts. See fossils. find animal sculptures or imagine Roman soldiers.

6 **Wimpole Way:** An ancient path through nearby villages and Wimpole Hall Estate. 12 miles in total however you can break this up.

7 **Finding Treasure.** Geocaching and treasure hunting. a fun way to get the kids out.

8 **Hayley Wood Bluebells.**. In spring. stroll through a local wood to see a mass of bluebells.

9 **Follow DNA! Hobson's Brook to Shelford.** Follow the water from Hobson's Brook to it's source and follow the cycle path to Shelford.

10 **Brampton Woods.** Ancient woodlands.

1   FEN DITTON & MILTON

Stourbridge Common to Fen Ditton and Milton Country Park. 1.5 hours. 5 miles. Alternatively, you can walk all the way to Waterbeach - 8 miles, 2.5 hours. A relatively flat

1. Start on **Midsummer Common** and head north to Riverside. Walk along the river, past the houseboats, the new bridge, and Cambridge Museum of Technology.

2. At the start of **Stourbridge Common** is a play park to your right. Follow the river north for a couple of miles. The path veers away from the river to the right, towards **Fen Ditton** and St Mary's Church and the King's Head Pub.

3. If you'd rather skip Fen Ditton you can carry on following the river.

4. If you go to Fen Ditton, you can finish here and take the path back or a bus.

5. Or if you like you can take a left down Church Street towards the **Plough**. Please take care with kids especially as the path ends and there are sections of road with no pavement. Near the Plough there is a recreation ground on the right or you can stop off at the pub for refreshments.

6. If you'd like to carry on to Milton Country Park, walk back

to the river along the main path and carry on heading north.

7. Cross under the A14 and carry on with the river to your left. There is a bridge over the river Cam shortly afterwards on the left.

8. (For a longer walk, you can carry on following the river to **Waterbeach.**)

9. Turn left onto the **Fen Road** and carry on until you get to the back of **Milton Country Park**, with Dickerson's Pit and Todd's Pit lakes. These are very steep gravel pit lakes, so keep children well away from the edge.

10. You can walk through the park and head back through the Science Park if you wanted to take a bus back into town.

Stourbridge common to Fen Ditton & Milton

© OpenStreetMap contributors

Stourbridge Common
to Waterbeach

© OpenStreetMap contributors

RIVER WALK TO GRANTCHESTER

This is a 3 mile walk following the river in the south of the city, and is one of the best walks around Cambridge. It is possible wheel a buggy along the cycle path route. A round trip on a straighter road back makes 5 miles in total.

1. You can start from **Lammas Land** or Grantchester Street. As you walk down the street there is a little Co-op shop where you can get supplies for the journey, especially drinks on a hot day.

2. *BUS:* The 18 bus goes from Drummer Street, Cambridge every hour, to Grantchester Street and Grantchester village.

3. Turn right onto Eltisley Avenue, past a chemist shop and then onto **Grantchester Meadows.** The houses gradually make way for grassy fenland. This is the start of the walk. The path is also known as the 'Grantchester Grind;.

4. There are two options, to keep on the more marked, higher path, or one closer to the river. In the summer, many people picnic by the banks of the river. The path continues on to Grantchester High Street.

5. This is the nicest part of the walk. You can watch the punts float by underneath the weeping willows.

6. The **Orchard Tea Rooms,** once the place of poets such as Byron and Rupert Brooke, has deckchairs under the apple trees for a tea and scone break.

7. *Return Jouney:* You can retrace your steps or go on the shorter route along Trumpington Road. After you reach Grantchester, keep left on Grantchester Road. Past the Mill Pond. The pavements can be narrow and winding.

8. After 50m take a right to Byron's Pool. Then back to Grantchester Road and turn right.

9. Follow the road as it forks, onto Church Lane and then left to Trumpington Road. Follow the pedestrian and cycle path back to Cambridge. It is a busy road but more direct.

BUS: To take the bus back, there are several along Trumpington Road. The 88 park and ride bus goes every 10 mins from a stop near Waitrose.

Grantchester Village

This ia a really pretty little village, with thatched cottages, a 14th century church. For refreshments try the local pubs the Blue Ball or Green Man, or sit outside in deck chairs under apple trees at the Orchard Tea Gardens.

Grantchester is said to have the highest concentration of Nobel Prize winners in the world. It is also a song by Pink Floyd, whose band members were from Cambridge. Recently it has been the setting for 'The Grantchester Mysteries' adapted for ITV drama.

There is a legend that there is a two mile old underground passage from the Old Manor House in Grantchester to King's College Chapel.

A fiddler was said to have volunteered to follow the passage. He set off, and the music from his playing became fainter and fainter and the stopped. He was never seen again.

Grantchester Meadows

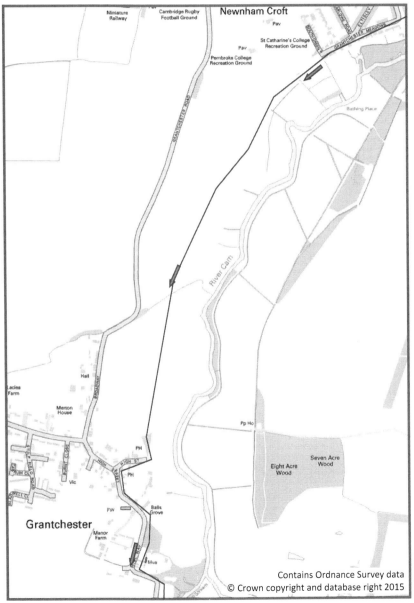

© Crown copyright and database right 2015
Contains Ordnance Survey data

ANGLESEY ABBEY WALK

1.5 hours, 4 miles. Around the beautiful Anglesey Abbey. You can visit the gardens too, which are lovely in the winter. Be careful as part of the route is very close to open water, and can be muddy. Dogs need to be on a lead near the

1. Drive to **Anglesey Abbey** on the B1102 Burwell Road. Park at the National Trust car park.

2. Head for the left hand corner of the car park, through a metal kissing gate, on to a narrow path to a recreation field. Go left behind the tennis court and past allotments to the right.

3. Turn left with backs of houses on the right to **Lode Mill.** Go over the footbridge and left along the river **Quy Water.** The Abbey gardens are on the other bank. Continue for one mile through **woodland**, see the old oak here, to open grass and through another metal kissing gate. Turn right along the hedge to the corner of the field.

4. Go through another kissing gate, a wooden one, turn sharp right along a grassy track as it turns left. Take the right fork and ago through another gate into a field, turn right and follow the sign to Lode (1 mile).

5. There is a **memorial stone** off the main path, for a William Ison who aged 29 got struck by lightening. Carry on the path past an old building to the right.

6. Turn right, follow the track behind the building, bear left in the middle of the wood and go back onto a field path which leads back to the **Mill**. Walk in front of the mill taking the NO HORSES path back to the car park.

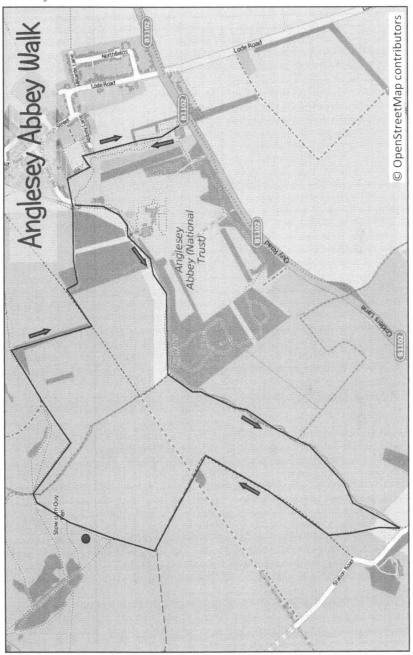

Anglesey Abbey Walk

ART & SCULPTURE

3 miles. 2 hours. A great way to see Cambridge, through some of the sculptures, paintings and buildings through the city centre. This starts from Kettle's Yard, around Jesus Green. It goes onto the sculptures in Jesus College and ending at the magnificent Fitzwilliam Museum.

1. Start at **Kettle's Yard,** Castle Street. This was founded by Jim Ede, former curator of the Tate gallery. As you leave and walk down Bridge Street, this area is one of the oldest in Cambridge and where early Roman and Normal settlers lived.

2. Turn left after the bridge, past the restaurants and punts onto the **wooden boardwalk.** In spring you can see the lovely college garden blossoms across the river to your left.

3. At the end of the boardwalk, turn left and keep along the river until you get to the kiosk and weir. Turn right down the avenue of **London Plane trees**, beautiful in the Autumn. Carry on until you get to the road.

4. Turn right and this will take you to the big entrance of **Jesus College.** Carry on past this, and turn right again down Jesus Lane to reach the second entrance to Jesus. If you go into the college you will find several interesting sculptures, including **Daedalus on Wheels** (Eduardo

Paolozzi) and the glass **Empress** (Danny Lane). Head out and carry on right down Jesus Lane, then next left down Malcom Street and then Hobson Street past the music shop on your right to **Christ's College.**

5. At Christ's College, go in and turn left utnil you get to the black door of the chapel, where you will find the painting **The Deposition** (Anthony Caro), then to the courtyard garden to find 'A

Pattern of Life' (Tim Harrison) and the **Darwin Garden sculpture.** The fellow's gardens here are very lovely if you would like to stroll around for longer.

6. Turn right out of the college, onto Hobson Street, but past Next and Boots to Market Street on the left. Carry on past the shops and the market to your left, and turn right at Rose Crescent. Follow this out onto Trinity and Garret Hostel Lane over the river to the Jerwood Library built in 1998.

7. Circle back to Senate Passage and turn right onto Kings Parade and enter **Clare College.** In the memorial court you will see the **DNA double helix sculpture** (Charles Jencks) to celebrate Crick and Watson's discovery of the structure of DNA. In the next court is a bronze Henry Moore from 1956, 'Fallen Warrior'.

8. As you come out of the college, follow Kings Parade to the **Corpus Clock** (sculpture by Matthew Lane Sanderson), created to represent the unstoppable nature of time.

9. Carry on walking along Trumpington Street and turn right onto **Downing Street**, and go right into the Museum of Archaeology and Anthropology to find the bronze feet. These are by

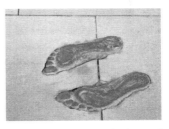

Anthony Gormley, he buried a full scale model of himself upside down and called it Earthbound.

10. Circle back on yourself to rejoin Trumpington Street, turn left and on the right is the fabulous **Fitzwilliam Museum**. This is full of art treausres, from classical sculputres, Matisse, Picasso, Barbara Hepworth, beautiful china and jewellery and more. The entrance of the museum is very grand and majestic. It is the main despository for the University of Cambridge works.

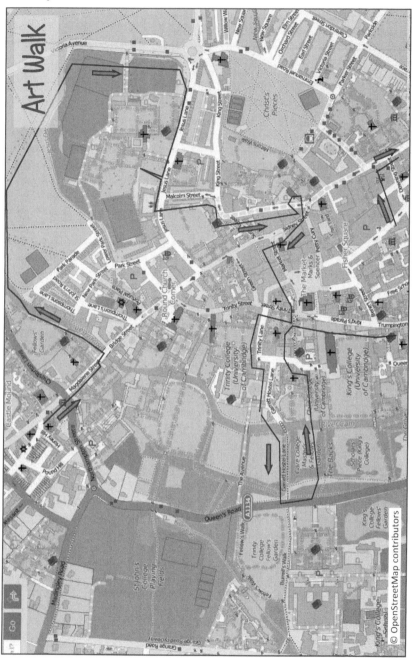

Art Walk

5 ANIMALS, FOSSILS, ROMANS

See the city in a new light, as you stroll around it. Awaken your child's interest in the stories behind places. Can you find sea creatures millions of years old at the shops? Imagine ice age mammoths on Cambridge City Football Ground?

Fossils at the shops!

www.sedgwickmuseum.org
The Sedgwick Museum of Earth Sciences has a great guide to rock types and geological features in our every day environment. You can

purchase it at the Museum. There are **cuttle fish** on the floor at Grand Arcade, millions of years old! It is clad in Jaumont

Limestone from France, and Jura Yellow Marble limestone.
Volcanic rock at Marks & Spencer? The store is clad from magma (formed from hot rock) of white & red granite and black gabbro.

Mammoths and Football

Cambridge City Football Ground used to be called **Swan's Pit**. It was a sand gravel quarry, and most of the buildings are made from this material.

Fossils of giant deer, mammoth, woolly rhino and horse were found here, dated 180,000 years ago, in the Ice Age.

Newmarket Road is also a site of fossils, of about 20,000 years old. At this time in the last Ice Age, ice sheets had ramped up on the North Norfolk coast, making the Cambridge area a very chilly ice-bound, high arctic environment. You can see the remains of these animals in the Sedgwick Museum.

The Romans and Saxons

Cambridge originated at the site of **Castle Hill.** The Romans under Govenor Scapula resisted fenland 'Iceni' and built a fort here, called **'Duroliponte'.** There are two city Roman roads: Akeman Street to the Fens and Via Devana northwest to Godmanchester.

The river used to be known as the Granta and the Saxons named it **'Grantabrycge'** (bridge of the Granta) and built St Benet's Church. The area grew as a Scandinavian trading centre and as an inland port. Imagine the boats by the river bustling with life and people.

Cambridge Castle

The Norman's built a Castle on the hill in 1068, but now just the mound remains. Climb up and you can see for miles, over King's College, Great St. Mary's Church and beyond to the flat fen landscape. If you look at the city coat of arms you'll see ships, sea horses and a castle.

Ancient Rivers

At the entrance to Jesus Green Swimming Pool you would have been under water thousands of years ago. There is a buried channel 10-15 metres deep. It runs beneath Jesus College, past Cambridge City football ground and north towards the Histon Road. There is also an old ridge of gravel starting from behind the old Leper Chapel on Newmarket Road to the Grafton Centre, which is the course of an old eastern tributory of the River Cam.

Hobson's Conduit

After disease and plague from unsanitary conditions, early in the 1600s the town and the University joined to fund Hobson's Conduit.

It's a watercourse that brings fresh water into the city.

The water comes from Nine Wells, which are springs at the foot of the Gog Magog hills near Great Shelford. This water is naturally filtered through the chalk rock, into Vicar's Brook. The octagonal monument shown, once formed part of the Market Square Fountain, and was moved to Lensfield Road corner after a fire in the Market in 1856.

The original courseway still functions along Trumpington Street, where it is known as Pem (east side) and Pot (west side).Thomas Hobson made lots of

money on horse traffic between Cambridge and London.

The expression 'Hobson's Choice' means that you've got 'no choice'. It was because he rented horses to students who had no choice about which horse they got.

Cambridge Train Station

The railway arrived in 1845, and placed outside the town centre following pressure from the University who restricted travel of undergraduates. In one year it was used by 8.8 million passengers (2011/12).

Elizabeth Way Bridge

In the 19th century, because of drops in wages and more mechanisation in the countryside, many people flocked to nearby towns like Cambridge to work on the pits, building colleges and the railway. Most of the housing was in East Road and Newmarket Road, which was cramped and in a poor state, lived in by manual labourers. Most of these houses have now been pulled down. The roundabout was where the village of Barnwell existed. Part of Barnwell Priory still exists on Beche Rd.

Did you know?

Parker's Piece is named after a college cook, Edward Parker, who obtained the rights to farm it. It was here that the Cambridge Rules of modern football were first put into practice.

Midsummer Common is common land. The Midsummer Fair is held every year and is one of the oldest fairs in the UK. It was granted a charter by King John in 1211. Cows are still allowed to graze there.

Christ's Pieces were originally owned by Jesus College. In 1574 it was used to grow cereal. In 1886, the area was acquired by the Corporation of Cambridge for the sum of £1,000. It is now a busy and well used park. Milton's walk is a medieval lane and is named after the poet John Milton, who was an undergraduate of Christ's College.

Coe Fen / Lammas Land / Sheep's Green

There were once up to three watermills in the area. The artificially raised banks of the watercourses are liable to flooding and only suitable for grazing (hence name Sheep's Green).

FEET, BISON AND A MAMMOTH

There are several sculptures, carvings and engravings around Cambridge, as well as interesting emblems of animals. They can be nice to look out for with kids when you are out and about. The colleges have gargoyles and Kings, Bishops and clocks. Younger kids may like seeing which animals they can find. Older children may appreciate the stories behind some of these objects. It can make walks around town a bit more interesting.

Some of my favourites are: Mammoth, Iguanadon, Bears, skeleton of Whale, wooden Mother and Child and Earthbound, (the 'upside down' feet - which is a whole statue of a man upside down). And that is just Downing Street!

Look out for the three Cambridge Sculpture Trail Guides, available free at the Tourist Office or online from Council City Council Sculpture Guides - www.cambridgesculpturetrails.co.uk

The Swimmers - Betty Rea
Parkside Pool

Confucius - Wu Wei Shah
Clare College

DOWNING STREET

There are many animal and people sculptures on Downing Street, see if you can find them.

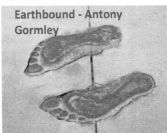

Earthbound - Antony Gormley

🦶🦶6 WIMPOLE WAY & COTON

12 miles in total however you can break this up into smaller chunks. The route goes through Coton, Hardwick, Caldecote and Kingston. Although there are parts, over a bridge and next to a road that you may want to miss. It can get muddy in places. It follows ancient trackways dating back to Anglo Saxon times.

Cambridge to Hardwick

1. The start of the walk is down Burrels Walk across Grange Road from the Backs. Carry on to **Adams Road** and at the junction of Wilberforce Rd is the start of the **Coton Footpath.**

2. The footpath runs along fields, and then on a bridge over the M11. Carry on to the **Coton Church** and past Whitwell Farm on the left. There is a short walk through the village.

3. **Coton** means 'cottages', probably 5th or 6th century. The church is 12th Century and has two Norman windows and a Saxon front. It has a **memorial** to Andrew Downs - one of the scholars who wrote the 17th Century version of the Bible.

4. There is a bridle path that follows the '**Whitwell Way'** , across the road, along the Portway towards Hardwick.

5. The path doesn't go through the village but it carries on over the road towards Caldecote.

6. **Hardwick** means Sheep Farm and was once a large Benedictine monastery.

7. The church tower contains an old oak chest with the remains of a helmet and dagger. It used to get very flooded and isolated, the people were branded as 'poor and ignorant' by a curate in 1938 due to this.

8. **Hardwick Wood** belonged to the Bishop of Ely until 1599, and has bluebells, oxslip, dog's mercury and primroses growing underneath the hazel, maple and ash trees. There are refreshments here.

9. The path goes through Hardwick Wood with Wood Barn Farm a way to the left until it gets to **Caldecote**.

10. This village has been in existence for a thousand years, since 1086. The name means Cold Cottages.

11. There are ancient tracks all around the village, which is spaced out along an old road.

Cambridge to Coton (Wimpole Way)

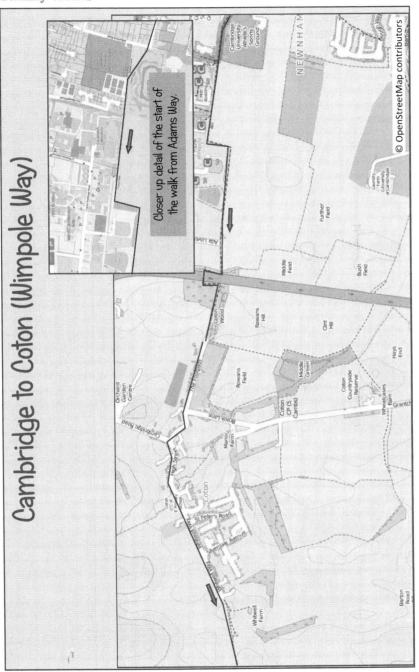

Closer up detail of the start of the walk from Adams Way.

© OpenStreetMap contributors

Coton to Hardwick (Wimpole Way)

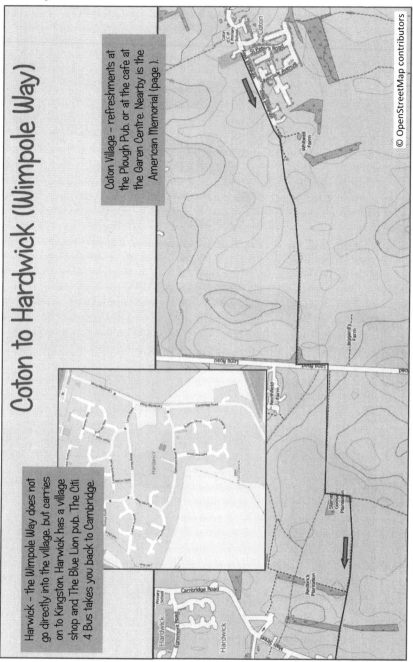

Coton Village – refreshments at the Plough Pub. or at the cafe at the Garen Centre. Nearby is the American Memorial (page).

Harwick – the Wimpole Way does not go direly into the village. but carries on to Kingston. Harwick has a village shop and The Blue Lion pub. The Citi 4 Bus takes you back to Cambridge.

© OpenStreetMap contributors

84

Wimpole Hall to Kingston

5.5 miles, 2.5 hours. (Circle 10 miles, 5 hours).

1. Start at **Wimpole Hall.** As you drive past the gates, notice these are carved with a stag and a lion from the coat of arms of the Earls of Hardwicke. Carry on past a big chestnut tree and tarmac drive past the front of Wimpole Hall. There are sometimes horned cattle in the field to the right, past the brick stable block. Park in the car park. Wimpole was once a medieval settlement, however it is now the site of the grand 18th Century mansion.

2. From the **stables**, walk across the lawns, go past the front of the Hall to the swing gate into the park. Go around to the right and then bear left through the avenue of trees. At the top of the hill, turn right through the

kissing gate. After a short while, bear left into the **woodlands.** Follow the signs north to Kingston on green metal signs near the road, yellow signs in the footpaths.

3. Be careful when the footpath meets the road after the Folly and towards Eversden Wood and Crane's Lane.

4. After crossing the road follow the bidleway to **Kingston** on the **Crane's Lane Bridlepath.**

5. Kingston means 'King's Farm' and indicates it was under royal ownship. It used to have an annual fair on the green which was 10 acres.

1. The **Church at Kingston** has some very find medieval wall paintings. You can stop for refreshments here and take the bus or circle back to the car park.

Wimpole Hall to Kingston

© OpenStreetMap contributors

7   TREASURE HUNTING

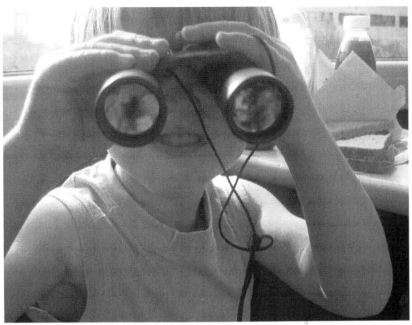

Geocaching

www.geocaching.com

This is a modern day treasure hunt, using a GPS device to find hidden containers or 'caches'.

It is a nice, simple idea set up by volunteers worldwide. And it's free. You can put in your postcode and search for nearby caches. You can also find out how to hide your own cache using the guidelines online.

They will contain a log book to sign, and a small number of items of low monetary value that you can trade e.g. Key rings, small toys.

Treasure Trails Cambridgeshire

www.treasuretrails.co.uk

A commercial website where you can buy trail maps and explore on a treasure hunt. In Cambridge there is a Riverside Walk, two College trails, a Ghost Story Trail and one from the train station to the city. Also Grantchester, Ely, Huntingdon.

8 HAYLEY WOOD BLUEBELLS

1.3 miles. 40 minutes. A short walk in woodlands. It is one of the most pretty woodlands around Cambridge. This one is notable for it's rare oxlips and bluebells in the spring. 8 miles

Hayley Wood is on the left after the village of Longstowe on the B1046. Park on the left hnd verge opposite the water tower. The hedge on Hayley Lane is 800 years old.

2. There are rare oxlips and bluebells. Oxlips are members of the primula family. There are also roe and muntjac deer in the countryside and there is a fence around the wood to keep them from eating all the flowers.

3. Walk down the track and pass a house on the left, which used to be the old railway worker house when the Cambridge to Oxford railway line passed through here. Keep straight ahead with the wood to the right, turn right at next side path (easy to miss) and cross a wooden bridge. The deer fence should be to your right. Go through metal gate and turn left on another path. Exit the wood at another metal gate and turn right along the edge of the wood, passing a field barn and retrace your steps.

4. There is an information shelter with views into the trees if you want to visit that. There is a memorial plaque to a Lancaster Bomber and it's people who crashed here in 1943 on return from a raid in Berlin. All crew were lost.

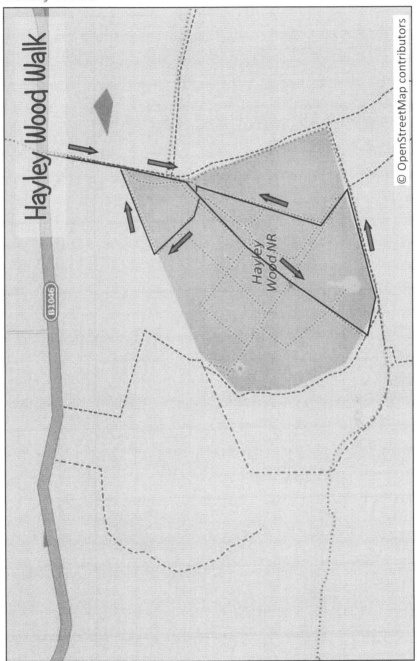

Hayley Wood Walk

Hayley Wood NR

B1046

© OpenStreetMap contributors

9 HOBSON'S BROOK

4 miles, 1.5 hours. Follow the Water to the Source. Vicar's Brooke, Addenbrookes and the Double Helix. You can do this walk all together or in two parts: Hobson's Conduit to Long Road; Addenbrookes to Great Shelford. Mainly flat. The last stretch is buggy friendly but the first part may be tricky by the brook and along the field.

1. You can follow the water that flows into Cambridge on the old **Hobson's Brook.**

2. Start on the corner of Lensfield Road and Trumpington Street (A1134) by **Hobson's Conduit.** Follow the stream by keeping it to your left. It goes past the **Botanic Garden** and feeds the lake there. Carry on until you get to the Brooklands Avenue. The map overleaf starts from Booklands Avenue.

3. Cross over the road. You'll need to head into the trees and follow the stream on the back of the allotments. It is nice and quiet here, just the bubbling brook and the fields beyond.

4. The small stream will join with **Vicar's Brook** which runs all the way to Lammas Land in Cambridge. Follow the stream towards Long Road.

5. Cross the road here at Addenbrookes Hospital, it has changed a lot in recent years with the addition of new buildings. You used to be able to follow the brook along here but there has been a lot fo contruction work.

6. **Addenbrooke's Hospital** is a world-renowned teaching

90

hospital with strong affiliations to the University of Cambridge. It was founded in 1766 on Trumpington Street from the will of Dr John Addenbrooke, a fellow of St Catharine's College. It moved to it's present place in 1976. The old building is now the Judge Business School.

7. The Cambridge Busway also operates here and cuts across the brook.

8. Whilst there is building work, you may have to veer off following the brook and instead head into the Hospital site. Follow the road into the sight until you get to a mini roundabout, take the **Francis Crick Avenue**, and veer left onto the Cycle path instead of over the trainline. It is from here that you can follow the flat cycle way to Shelford.

9. After a short way, there is a short detour to **Nine Wells**, which is the source of the water for Hobson's Brook.

10. The series of strips in four colours represent the 10,257

genetic letters of the gene **BRCA2** are laid on the cycle path using themoplastic strips heat welded onto the tarmac. Green is adenine, blue is cytosine, yellow is guanine and red is thymine - the code for life. BRCA2 is just one of the 30,000 genes in the human genome, producing protein to help repair DNA, but variants can cause breast cancer.

11. It goes all the way to Great Shelford, with a **DNA Double Helix sculpture** marking the end of the path. Follow the path and go over the railway crossing on Granham's Road.

12. Carry on until the A1301 onto Tunwells Lane which will take you into the heart of the town. There are a couple of nice cafes and pubs if you want refreshments here.

13. If you want to take the train back from **Shelford,** turn left at the traffic lights onto Station Road.

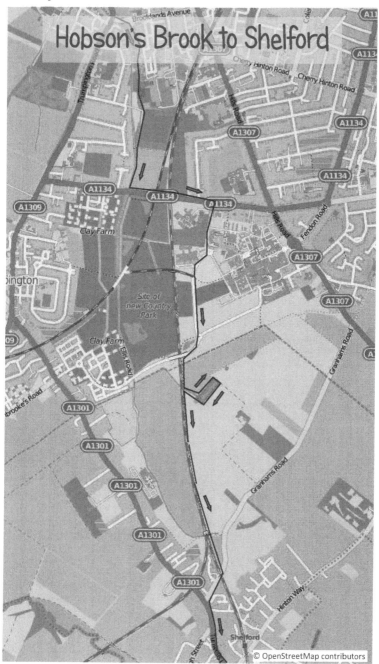

Hobson's Brook to Shelford

10   BRAMPTON WOOD

It is about 4 miles , 1.5 hours.This is the second largest ancient woodland in Cambridgeshire, being over 900 years old. The trees are oak, yew, ash, field maple and birch. In the spring it is full of bluebells. There are primrose, wood spurge and common spotted orchid flowers. It is 4 miles south west of Huntingdon. Map Reference TL 184 698

1. You can park by the entrance. There are a choice of paths, you could walk around the perimeter or head into the centre.
2. Note the fine two oak trees near the entrance, and are known as 'The Sentinel or Master Oaks'.
3. Keep walking on the main path straight into the woods. Nearby are a group of wild cherry trees and 'chequer' trees that were once used to make fermented drinks.
4. At the crossroads there is a great view of the 'main' and 'cross' rides or paths. There is a crab apple tree nearby.
5. Turn left onto the 'cross ride' and over a stream. Walk until you get the perimeter of the woods. If you then turn right to follow the outside of the trees, you will see the two old wild pear trees.
6. Keep walking around the woods past the turning for the 'west ride', keep to the outside of the

woods on the public bridleway and over the stream. There are Muntjac deer and 'Black Hairstreak ' butterflies, one of the rarest in the UK. These butterflies have orange tinges on the wings and a brown body.
7. As you reach the furthest corner, carry on to the right. This is the best place to see bluebells.
8. Turn right into the 'cross ride' path, to the cross roads again.
9. Turn left towards the public car park again.

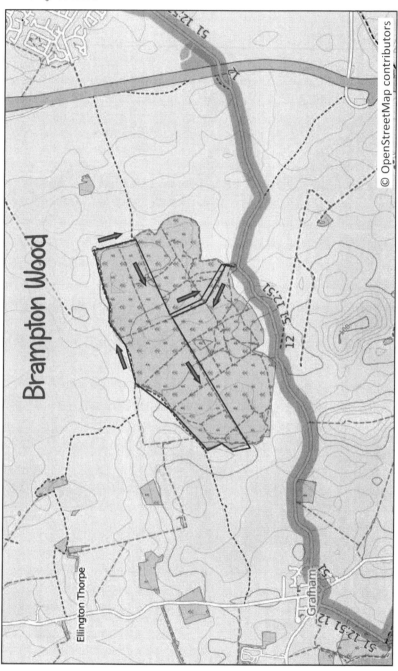

Family Days Out

Outside Cambridge, there are plenty of pretty villages, historic houses and nature reserves. Nearby wildlife parks such as Shepreth, and activity centres such as Go Ape are great for families too. Discover Norman and Saxon England at the Fort at Stansted Mountfitchet.

Anglesey Abbey has beautiful gardens. Ely and Peterborough Cathedral are magnificent. Hinchingbrooke House, Kimbolton Castle, Buckden Towers, Elton Hall and Wimpole Hall are also worth a trip out.

The sweeping, marsh lands make beautiful country parks, such as Wicken Fen, Nene Park, Flag Fen, Wandlesbury Country Park, Brampton Wood, the Ouse Valley, Wicken Fen, Paxton Pits and Grafham Water.

Because the area is very flat, many airfields were built here, such as RAF Bomber and Fighter Command in World War II. See the planes at the Imperial War Museum at Duxford. Or take a miniature train at Audley End.

Nearby towns such as Newmarket, Ely, St Ives and Huntingdon have their own attractions, such as horse racing. There is even a cave to explore at Royston!

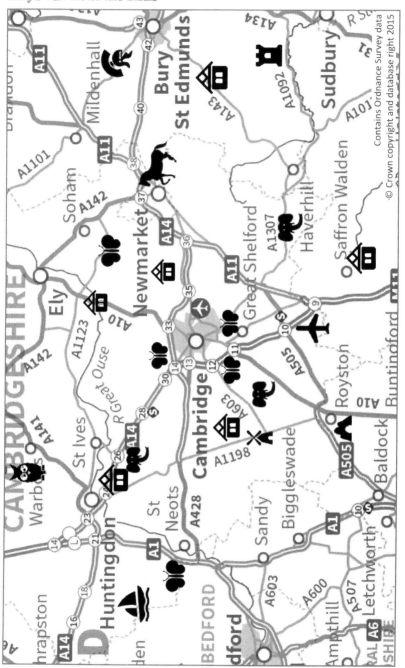

Attractions within 10 miles of Cambridge

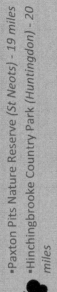

- Milton Country Park - 2 miles
- Wandlebury Country Park (south) - 4 miles
- Coton Countryside Reserve (south) - 5 miles
- Anglesey Abbey (half way to Ely) - 6 miles
- Denny Abbey and Farmland Museum (beyond Waterbeach)- 8 miles
- Wimpole Hall Estate (south of Cambridge) - 8 miles
- Bourne Postmill - 9 miles
- Shepreth Wildlife Park - 7 miles
- Linton Zoo - 10 miles

Within 20 miles of Cambridge

- Duxford Imperial War Museum (Whittlesford) - 13 miles
- St Ives - 14 miles
- Hinxton Watermill (Saffron Walden) - 15 miles
- The Manor (Hemingford Grey) - 16 miles
- Huntingdon (incl: Houghton Water Mill) - 18 miles
- Audley End House (Saffron Walden) - 19 miles
- Ely (including Cathedral) - 17 miles

- Newmarket (including Horse Museum, Brandon Park, Hill Lodge/Go Ape & Wild Tracks) - 18 miles
- Wicken Fen Nature Reserve (near Ely) - 18 miles
- Paxton Pits Nature Reserve (St Neots) - 19 miles
- Hinchingbrooke Country Park (Huntingdon) - 20 miles
- The Raptor Foundation (near Warboys)- 20 miles
- Royston (including Royston Cave) - 20 miles

Within 30 miles of Cambridge

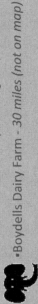

- Ouse Washes Nature Reserve (March/Ely) - 24 miles
- Hitchin Lavender - 26 miles
- Welney Wetlands Reserve (beyond Ely) - 26 miles
- Grafham Water (Huntingdon) - 25 miles
- St. Mary's Church (Buckdon) - 25 miles
- Clare Castle Country Park (near Sudbury) - 26 miles
- Ickworth House Park and Gardens (Bury St Edmunds) - 29 miles
- Hamerton Zoo Park (Hunttingdon) - 30 miles
- Boydells Dairy Farm - 30 miles (not on map)

Map of Cambridgeshire

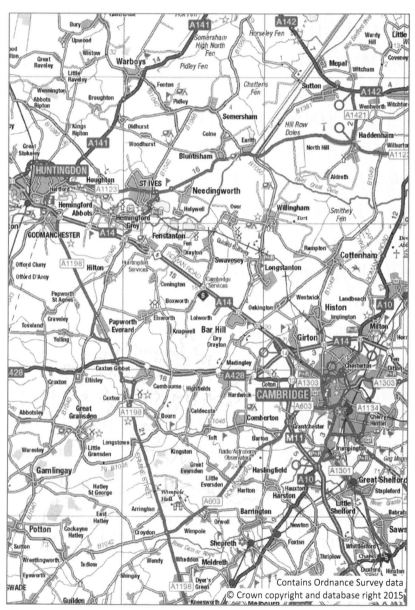

Contains Ordnance Survey data
© Crown copyright and database right 2015

Animals & Wildlife

Linton Zoo – 10 miles (from Cambridge

Exotic animals like tarantulas, giant tortoises, hornbills, toucans, parrots and snow leopards, Sumatran tigers and zebra.

It also has gardens with Tasmanian giant tree ferns and a cafe.

Hadstock Rd, Linton, Cambridge, CB21 4NT
Tel: 01223 891308
enquiries@lintonzoo.co.uk
www.lintonzoo.com
Open: Check website as this varies, usually 10:30-4pm/5pm or 6pm in summer holidays.
Admission: Adult £9.00, child £6.50

Getting there: Bus - 45 minutes. Bus X13 to Linton, walk 15 mins. **Car** - 23 minutes (10 miles)

Shepreth Wildlife Park – 8 miles

This includes lemurs, meerkats and a tiger. See the waterworld, nocturnal house, farm animals and wolves. Take a walk through bunny land. There are regular feeding sessions and a birds of prey display. There is also a cafe, a playground with a pirate ship and a bug city world. It is handy to get to by train.

Willersmill, Station Road, Shepreth, SG8 6PZ
Tel: 01763 262226
www.sheprethwildlifepark.co.uk
Open: 10am-6pm in Summer, 10am-4pm Winter (last entry one hour before)
Admission: Wildlife park only - Adults £11.95 Children £9.95 (<2 yrs free)

Getting there: Car - off A10 between Cambridge and Royston, or the **train** to Shepreth (it's right by the station)

Hamerton Zoo Park – 30 miles

See the cheetah, owls, white tiger and monkeys at this Park near Sawston. There are two play areas, babies and toddlers and older kids and covered picnic areas. A cafe and shop. The stroll-a-safari allows you to get up close to the animals.

Hamerton, Sawtry PE28 5RE
Tel: 01832 293362
www.hamertonzoopark.com/
Open: 10.30am - 6pm in the summer and 10.30am - 4pm in the winter. Times change with the clocks.
Admission: Adults - £11.95
Children - £7.95 (3 to 12)

Getting there: Car 1 hour (30 miles) via A14 to Huntingdon.

Animal Centres

Boydells Dairy Farm – 30 miles

A small working farm run by the Treadgold family, specialising in sheep milking. It has hens and even llamas. You can take a guided tour and even try milking a cow or sheep. You can also ride a donkey cart.

Wethersfield, Braintree, Essex CM7 4AQ
Tel: 01371 850481
enquiries@boydellsdairy.co.uk

www.boydellsdairy.co.uk
Open: 14:00-17:00 Fri, Sat and Sun and Bank Holidays.
Admission: Adults £5.00, Child £4.00

Getting there: Bus/Train - 3 hours. Train to Stansted Airport, Bus 133 to Braintree, Bus 10 to Shalford, Boydells . **Car** - 1 hour (30 miles)

The Raptor Foundation – 20 miles

The foundation provides sanctuary, care and rehabilitation for birds. Here you will find many species of raptors. There is a tea room, pond, shop, exhibition and play area. The place runs experience days like the falconry day and hawk walk, as well as photography activities.

The Heath, St Ives Road, Woodhurst, Huntingdon, Cambridgeshire, PE28 3BT
Tel: 01487 741140
info@raptorfoundation.org.uk
www.raptorfoundation.org.uk

Open: 10:00-17:00 in summer, check website for details.

Admission: Adult £6.05 Child £3.85

Getting there: Bus - 1 hour 10 minutes. Busway A to Wytoon Airfield, Bus 30 to Old Hurst, Bus 22 to Woodhurst. **Car** - 45 minutes (20 miles).

Wood Green Animal Shelter - 17 miles

Provides Shelter and care for up to 6,000 domestic animals every year. Set in 52 acres of countryside. Some larger breeds such as llamas and deer are permanent residents. There are weekend events and a cafe.

Visitors are welcome to the shop and cafe but access to the kennels is restricted to those who are genuinely looking to rehome a dog.

London Road, Godmanchester, Cambs. PE29 2NH
Tel: 08701 90 40 90
www.woodgreen.org.uk
Open: 10:00-16:00 Tuesday to Sunday.
Admission: Free

Getting there: Train - 1 hour, Huntingdon nearest (10 minutes by taxi). **Car** - 35 minutes (17 miles).

Further Afield

Banham Zoo - 50 miles

Over 2000 animals in nearly 50 acres of park and gardens. Cafe and visitor centre. Zebras, giraffes, Leopards, monkeys, penguins and birds. Also a Skytrek activity.

Kenninghall Road, Banham, Norfolk NR16 2HE
Tel: 01953 887771
www.banhamzoo.co.uk
Open: Daily from 9:30am. Oct-mar last admission -b3pm; Mar to July - 4pm; July & Aug 5pm; Oct - 4pm.
Admission: Peak days Adult £18.10, Child £12.65. Under 3s free.

Getting there: Bus/Train -not really accessible, closest Train is Norwich, 1 hour to Norwich, 1 hour by Bus 10A at least from Norwich to Banham. **Car** - 1 hour 30 minutes (50 miles)

Exotic Pet Refuge - 40 miles

Founded in 1984, the Exotic Pet Refuge is a small charity that gives home to all kinds of animals.

Note: NOT open to the general public. It has special open times only 6 days a year. Please check website before visiting.

102 Station Road, Deeping St. James, Peterborough PE6 8RH
Tel: 01778 345 923
www.exoticpetrefuge.org.uk

Planes, War & Trains

Imperial War Museum Duxford –

9 miles

Regular air shows and famous military aircraft. Collections of tanks, military vehicles and artillery. There are great aerial displays from spitfires and other World War planes at their regular events. These are held usually in Spring, Summer and Autumn. It has three cafés on site - The Mess Restaurant, Wing Co Joes Café and Station 357.

Duxford, Cambridgeshire CB22 4QR
Tel: 01223 835000
Open: Daily, Winter 10:00-16:00 (last admission 15:00), Summer 10:00-18:00 (last admission 17:00).
Admission: Adult £17.50; Child (under 16) free

Getting there: Car - Just south of Cambridge at Junction 10 of the M11 motorway. On Sundays there is a direct Myalls 132 bus service from Cambridge to air shows.

American Military Cemetary – 4 miles

The Memorial site was donated by the University of Cambridge. There are nearly 4,000 servicemen buried here and 5,127 names are recorded on the Tablets of the Missing. Most died in the Battle of the Atlantic or in the strategic air bombardment of northwest Europe.

A moving monument, with a reflecting pool and the Tablets of the Missing.

Coton, Cambridge CB23 7PH
Open: 9 - 5 pm, except December 25 and January 1
Getting there: Car - 3 miles west of Cambridge on the A1303, near Coton.

Audley End Miniature Railway – 16 miles

Steam trains and fairies and elves. You can take a walk through the woods to spot the Fairies and Elves hiding in their tree houses. It has a large picnic area with a wooden playground. Check the website for special train days. You can get snacks at the Signal Box Café.

Bruncketts, Wendens Ambo
Saffron Walden, Essex CB11 4JL
Tel: 01799 542134
enquiries@audley-end-railway.co.uk
www.audley-end-railway.co.uk
Open: 11am - 5pm. Railway - Weekends April to October. Fairy Walk - May - September & School Holidays.
Admission: Adult - £5.50; Child - £4.50. Under 2's go free. Combined tickets/specials varies – £8.00.

Getting there: By Car - One mile west of Saffron Walden on the B1282. Follow the brown tourist information signs to Audley End House. **By Train:** Nearest is Audley End Station. Approximately 1 mile from the Minature Railway.

Castles & Flowers

Stansted Mountfitchet Castle

An open air museum experience, where you can travel back in time to see what life was like in Norman times. You can dress up, wander about the chickens, see the log fires and feed the tame Fallow deer. Please note that it is steep in places, and access to the Bailey is up a 45 degree grassy slope, so wheelchairs or buggies may need to check first.

There is also a Hill Toy Museum included in the entry price, which has the largest collection of toys in the world. From the Victorian era to the present day. Here you can find the Haunted Manor with life sized dinosaurs and fossil hunting.

Stansted, Essex CM24 8SP
Tel: 01279 813237
info@mountfitchetcastle.com
www.mountfitchetcastle.co.uk
Open: March to October 10am-5pm including all weekends and Bank Holidays. (from Sunday 25th Oct the Castle & the Toy Museum will close at 4.00pm)
Admission: Adults £9.95, Children(3 13yrs) £7.95

Getting there: Car - 31 miles (40 minutes) 2 miles from Junction 8 off the M11, follow the brown tourist signs to Stansted Mountfitchet village.
Train - Castle is right next to Stansted Mountfitchet station - 35 minutes.

Hitchin Lavender

A farm with acres of Lavender in the summer months. There is also a wildflower and sunflower strip. There are bee hives and a shop.

You can wander around the lavender and pick a bunch to bring home.

Cadwell Farm, Hitchin, Hertfordshire SG5 3UA, United Kingdom
Tel: 01462 434343
www.facebook.com/HitchinLavender
Open: May to Aug Mon - Sun: 10–5pm
Admission: Check website.

Getting there: Car - 50 minutes (30 miles) Off A1 at junction 10, follow A507 towards Stotfold, then signs to Ickleford. Then on to Arelsey New Road, turn left to Hitchin Lavender.
Bus - Route 72. **Train** - 1 hour to Hitchin, but would need a taxi or Bus 53 or 72

Adventure

Mepal Outdoor Centre

Outdoor activity centre for all ages. It has a family Sundays such as climbing, kayaking and archery, day camps and training courses.

Chatteris Road, Nr Ely Cambs CB6 2AZ
Tel: 01354 692251
info@mepal.co.uk
www.mepal.co.uk

Getting there: Train to Ely then Bus 9 towards Chatteris. Would probably need a taxi for rest of the way. **Car** - 20 miles, 40 minutes off the A10 towards Ely, turn off at Strethem towards Sutton, then on the A142 north towards Chatteris.

Hill Lodge Forest Centre...

Lovely park with adventure play area and cafe. There is a 'superworm' trail, you can buy an activity pack for £3.50 at High Lodge with a trail and stickers.

& Go Ape! Forest Adventure

Try the Tree Top Adventure, Forest Segway and Junior Adventures (6 to 12 yrs over 1 metre tall).

Santon Downham, Brandon, Suffolk, IP27 0AF
Tel: 01842 815434
www.forestry.gov.uk/highlodge
http://goape.co.uk/days-out/thetford
Open: February to November.

Getting There - By car - from the A11 take the B1107 towards Brandon, and follow signs to High Lodge Forest Centre. **Train** - nearest train is Thetford. **Bus** - Mon to Fri between High Lodge, Brandon and Thetford.

Wild Tracks

An outdoor activity park with clay shooting, crossbows, archery, karting, quad bikes and junior activities. For ages 8 yrs upwards (1.3metres plus).

Chippenham Road, Kennett, Newmarket CB8 7QJ
Tel: 01638 751918
www.wildtracksltd.co.uk

Getting there: Car - 3 miles north of Newmarket and 20 minutes from Cambridge. Follow A11 to Norwich and turn off at second exit onto the B1085 sign for Offroad Activity Park.

Nature Reserves

Coton Countryside Reserve

The Cambridge Past, Present and Future Preservation Group (a local charity) have turned 27 acres of arable fields into accessible meadows with 4 miles of routes. Part of it is concrete and suitable for pushchairs, cycles and wheelchair users.

There is a visitor guide on the website, with marked paths, which are worth sticking to unless you want to end up on the rifle range! You can see Beetle banks, grassy mounds in the middle of fields to provide winter houses for insects and spiders, and Black Poplars, now one of the rarest native timber species in Britain.

Coton, Cambridgeshire
www.cambridgeppf.org/coton-countryside-reserve

Getting there: Bus - 15 minutes, Citi 4 towards Lower Cambourne. **Car** - 15 minutes (5 miles) on A1134 and A1303.

Ouse Washes Nature Reserve

The Ouse Washes is an excellent introduction to Fenland wildlife. In the winter, the reserve attracts thousands of ducks and swans; and redshanks, lapwings and snipe breed in the summer. Walking behind the banks avoids putting the wildfowl to flight. Good for people with an interest in birds. There are 10 hide's available and a visitor centre.

Welches Dam Manea, March PE15 0NF
Tel: 01354 680212
ouse.washes@rspb.org.uk
www.rspb.org.uk

Getting there: Train - 45 minutes. Change or take a taxi at Ely. Manea Station is 5km from the reserve (no

Sunday trains). **Car** - 1 hour 15 minutes (32 miles).

Paxton Pits Nature Reserve

75 hectares of gravel pits, meadows, scrub and woodland next to the River Great Ouse. There is a wealth of wildlife to enjoy all year round, and a network of marked paths. During May there are large numbers of Nightingales and many species of orchid in the meadows.

The Visitor Centre has a childrens corner, with activities and a nature table, including mammoth finds from the quarry. There is a cafe here too.

Little Paxton, Huntingdon PE19 4ET.
Tel: 01480 406795
Open: Daily. A Visitor Centre is open most weekends, with Volunteer Wardens, leaflets, maps and refreshments.

Getting there: Car - 35 minutes (19 miles) on A428. **Train** - St Neots it is 2 miles from the station along the Ouse Valley Way.

Fishing - Cloudy, Rudd and Hayling Lakes Little Paxton Fisheries.
Permits from Ouse Valley Specialist Angling, 25-31 Huntingdon Street, St Neots.
Tel: 01480 386088

Sailing - Paxton Lakes Sailing Club
Tel: 01707 322141

Waterskiing - South Lake Ski School
Tel: 01480 216966

Wicken Fen Nature Reserve

This is Britain's oldest nature reserve. It is a unique fragment of the wilderness that once covered East Anglia. The Fen is a haven for birds, plants, insects and mammals alike. There are grazing herds of Highland cattle and Konik ponies which are creating new habitats. It can be explored by the traditional wide droves and lush green paths and nature trailhides. The boardwalk is suitable for buggies and wheelchairs, and is 1.2 km long (50 minutes).

It also has a visitor centre and cycle hire. There are lots of family events held regularly and even wild camping under the stars (you will need to book ahead). And there are also boat trips for a peaceful cruise on the 'Mayfly' (50 minutes, family ticket £16).

There is a willow tunnel play area next to the cafe, child bikes, tags and trailers for hire. There are also ten secret geocaches on the reserve for those seeking hidden treasure.

Lode Lane, Wicken, Ely, CB7 5XP
Tel: 01353 720274
wickenfen@nationaltrust.org.uk
www.wicken.org.uk
Open: 10:00-17:00 daily.
Admission: Adult £6.45, Child £3.15, Family £16.00

Getting there: Car - 40 minutes (18 miles). **Train** - not really accessible, 9 miles from Ely Station.

Welney Wetland Centre

A National Trust site, and one of the most important wetlands in Europe. It is also home to the National Dragonfly Centre. Herons, cormorants, many ducks and geese, dragonflies, butterflies and wild flowers. It has a Visitor Centre and Cafe. 850 acre wildfowl reserve including nature trail.

There is a pond room with art and craft activities, a main observatory to watch the birds and dragonfly ponds. If you have binoculars, bring them along! It helps to see the wildlife if you are quiet and approach the hides slowly.

Hundred Foot Bank, Welney, Nr.Wisbech PE14 9TN
Tel: 01353 860711
info.welney@wwt.org.uk
www.wwt.org.uk
Open: 10am-5pm daily;Ater pm Thursdays to Sundays in the summer.

Getting there: Train - Ely and then bus (9 miles from train). **Car** - By road 17 miles north-east of Cambridge via A10

Spring

This is nest building time for birds, see if you can spot them in the trees. Listen to the bird songs, cuckoos, woodpeckers, pigeons, blackbirds and crows. Find frogspawn in ponds, and see the catkins, blossom, bluebells and daffodils bloom.

Summer

Look out for ants, see how they follow a trail and carry leaves many times bigger than themselves. Bees and cabbage white butterflies are hovering around the flowers. Yellow dandelions, daisies and buttercups are on the meadows. On a hot day in the grass, you may be able to hear grasshoppers. Ladybirds help to eat the green aphids which attack plants.

Autumn

A great time to go on acorn, conker and pine cone hunts and run through russet red fallen leaves. Squirrels will be collecting for their winter store. Spiders and their webs are comon. There are also mushrooms growing in grasslands and around trees.

Winter

See which trees and bushes have lost their leaves, and which are evergreen, like holly, ivy and pines. Hedgehogs and bats hibernate, other animals have to find shelter.

Houses & Gardens

Anglesey Abbey

House built in 1600 on the site of a 12th-century priory, with a collection built by Huttleston Broughton, 1st Lord Fairhaven. There is nearly 100 acres of landscape garden and arboretum with over 100 pieces of sculpture.

There is a winter walk and snowdrops n January and February, hyacinths in the spring, herbaceous borders and dahlia gardens in the summer and magnificent autumn foliage.

The working watermill regularly mills grain for sale. Hip-carrying infant seats for loan (available in the house), a Children's quiz/trail, family adventure packs. There is a great tree house to get a birds eye view of the Wildlife Discover Area for kids.

Garden & Lode Mill, Quy Road, Lode, Cambridgeshire CB25 9EJ
Tel: 01223 810080
angleseyabbey@nationaltrust.org.uk
www.nationaltrust.org.uk/anglesey-abbey
Open: See website, different times for house, gardens and mill. Gardens generally 10:30-17:30 in summer.
Admission: Gardens only Adult £7.10 Child £3.75, Family £16.85. Whole Property Adult £11.60, Child £6.00, Family £29.50.

Getting there: Car - 6 miles north east of Cambridge on B1102. Signposted from A14 (jct. 35). **By Foot** - Harcamlow Way from Cambridge. **Cycle** - NCN51, 1¼ miles. **Bus** - Stagecoach route 10 from Cambridge Bus Station.

108

Audley End House & Gardens

An insight into Victorian life. The house has elaborately decorated rooms and an art collection. Stables with horses and a Victorian groom. Also a service Wing including kitchen, scullery, pantry and laundries, gives you an insight into Victorian life below stairs. Originally adapted from a medieval Benedictine monastery, the house and gardens at Audley End were amongst the largest and most opulent in Jacobean England.

Parkland designed by "Capability" Brown. Fine formal Victorian gardens in process of being restored to their former glory. Walled organic kitchen garden stocked to match the 1800's plants. River Cam dammed to provide artificial lake.

There are two cafes, one with a playground next to it. Extensive grassed areas idea for family activities. Bike stands available by Lion Gates, but please do not ride bikes inside the grounds. Kites are welcome. Sling Loan on request.

Off London Road, Saffron Walden, Essex, CB11 4JF
Tel: 01799 522842
www.english-heritage.org.uk/daysout/properties/audley-end-house-and-gardens
Open: See website as these change. Usually term time Saturday and Sunday 10-4pm, School Holidays open all week.
Admission: Adult £16.00, Child (5-15 yrs) £9.60, Family (2 Adults, 3 children) £41.60

Getting there: **Bus** - Burton/Four Counties 59, Stansted Transit 301 from Audley Endrailway station stopping in Saffron Walden. By **Car** 1 mile W of Saffron Walden on B1383 (M11 exit 8 or 10). By **Train**, Audley End 1 1⁄4 miles. Note: Footpath is beside busy main road, 1.5 miles from the station.

Bourne Post Mill

One of the oldest surviving windmills in the country. Exterior can be visited any time during daylight, the inside on National Mills weekend (second Sunday in May) and last Sunday of the month in Summer. Check website to be sure.

Bourn Post Mill is located off Caxton Road, Bourn CB23 2SU between the villages of Bourn and Caxton.
www.cambridgeppf.org/bourn-post-mill
Getting there: Car - (9 miles) On the A428 from Cambridge take the turn after the blue footbridge signed Caldecote then follow Bourn Airfield and then Bourn, and take a right turn into Caxton Road. Alternatively turn off the A1198 at Caxton village. The mill is signed from the centre of the village.

Brandon Country Park

This was originally an Edwardian country house, and now it is a lovely park with lawns and a lake. There is a walled garden and apple orchard. There are Copper Beech tea rooms and a small shop and visitor centre.

Bury Road, Brandon, Suffolk
Tel: 01842 810185
www.brandoncountrypark.co.uk
Open: March to October: Monday to Friday from 10am until 5pm and Saturday to Sunday from 10am until 5.30pm
November to February: Daily from 10am until 3.30pm

Clare Castle Country Park

Extensive grounds and parkland around the ruins of 13th century Clare Castle. Several walks around the park, the river Stour, a nature trail, old station house and a visitor centre. It is in the picturesque, historic town of Clare, just two minutes walk from the town centre.

Maltings Lane, Clare, Suffolk CO10 8NJ
www.clare-uk.com/pages/clare-castle
country-park-602 **Admission:** Free

Getting there: **Car** - 50 minutes (26 miles). **Bus** - 1 hour 10 minutes, X13 to Haverhill, then 236 to Clare.

Denny Abbey and Farmland Museum

The Abbey is a 12th century building lived in by Benedictine monks, Franciscan nuns and Knights Templers. The farmland musem has a programme of events such as basket making, family history and children's activity days on school holidays. There is a farmworker's cottage, blacksmith, a dairy, fenman's hut and more. It has a cafe, picnic area, childrens play area and shop.

Ely Road, Waterbeach, Cambridge CB25 9PQ
Tel: 01223 860988
Info@farmlandmuseum.org.uk
www.dennyfarmlandmuseum.org.uk
Open: In the summer, April-October Weekends and bank holiday Mondays 10.30-17.00, weekdays 12.00-17.00 Closed November to March.
Admission: Adults £5.00, Child £3.00, Family £13.00.

Getting there: Car - 20 minutes (8 miles) on A10. **Bus** - Stagecoach 9 towards Chatteris, get off at Landbeach, Research Park Entrance, bus takes 30 minutes, walk 15 minutes.

Grafham Water

On the Northern Shore is an exhibition centre showing how the reservoir was built and a cafe. You can walk around the reservoir and you can also hire bikes from the centre.

Marlow Park, Grafham, Huntingdon, Cambridgeshire, PE28 0BH
Tel: 01480 812154
www.grafham-water-centre.co.uk

Getting there: Car - 40 minutes (25 miles) via A14, then exit at 23 to A1 and B661 to Ridgeway.

Hinchingbrooke Country Park

170 acre Country Park near Huntingdon. Free access to woods, lakes and meadows. Disabled access to visitor centre, toilets, hardened paths. Fishing platforms and wildlife garden. Electric wheelchairs available for

use. Watersports available to people of all abilities The house was originally a medieval nunnery converted by Cromwell family in the 16th century, later extended by the Earls of Sandwich.

Brampton Road, Huntingdon, Cambridgeshire, PE29 6DB
Tel: 01480 451568
www.huntingdonshire.gov.uk/Parks%20and%20Countryside/Hinchingbrooke%20Country%20Park/Pages/default
Open: All year.
Admission: Free for park. Pay for house.

Getting there: Bus - 1 hour 27 minutes, Busway A to Histon, then Busway B to Hinchingbrooke Park. **Train** - 1 hour 19 minutes, to Hitchin then Huntingdon then walk 15 mins. **Car** - 45 minutes (20 miles), A14 and A1.

Hinxton Watermill

he mill itself is situated on the River Cam with inner mill workings intact. It is found in the pretty village of Hinxton, constructed in 17th century.The exterior of the mill can be enjoyed at any time of the year from the riverside footpath. The mill is especially worth visiting on one of the summer open days, which are usually the first Sunday of the month (but check first).

Mill Lane, Hinxton CB10 1RD
www.cambridgeppf.org/hinxton watermill.shtml

Getting there: Car - 25 minutes (15 miles) via M11, then exit 10 to A505. Then take A1301 to Mill Lane. **Bus** - Citi 7 then Bus 7A, or

Ickworth House Park and Gardens

A lovely 1800 acre landscape with a Georgian Italianate palace. The Ickworth family and subsequent Lord Hervey's gave the house an interesting and eccentric history, full of intrigue. There are acres of woodland that can be explored by foot or by bike. It has a cafe and restaurant, gift shop, plant and garden centre. There are living history days, and events such as archery and out door theatre.

The Rotunda, Bury St Edmunds, IP29 5QE
Telephone: 01284 735270
ickworth@nationaltrust.org.uk
www.nationaltrust.org.uk/ickworth
Open: Varies. Gardens 10:00-17:30. Park dawn to dusk.

Admission: Whole property: Adult £12.60, child £6.35. **Park and gardens:** Adult £6.25 Family £15.65 **House up-grade** Adult £6.35, Child £3.10, Family £12.00.

Getting there: Train - Bury St Edmunds (3 miles from the Station). **Car** - 43 minutes (30 miles) near Bury St. Edmunds, follow A14 east.

Mildenhall Museum

The history of Mildenhall, has holiday activities for kids, and exhibits.

King Street, Mildenhall, Suffolk IP28 7EX
Tel: 01638 716970
www.mildenhallmuseum.co.uk
Open: Closed from Christmas until March. Open on Tues, Weds, Thur 2-

4.30pm, Fri 10.30-4.30pm; Sat 2-4.30pm.
Closed 4pm December.
FREE

Milton Country Park

A large park created from old gravel pits. The paths are suitable for bicycles and wheelchairs. Watch kids near the steep sided lakes. There is a Visitor Centre with café, two play-areas, a sensory garden and sunclock. There are also regular events such as the Halloween Twilight Walk and Easter Egg Hunt.

Milton, CB4 6AZ
www.miltoncountrypark.org
Open: All year.
Admission: Free.

Getting there: Car - Junction of the A10 and A14 to Milton Village.

Oliver Cromwell's House

Domestic life in the 17th Century in a variety of re-created period rooms as well an exhibition detailing the Civil War. See Mrs Cromwell's kitchen, try dressing-up or playing with the toys of the time or venture into the Haunted Bedroom.

29 St Mary's Street, Ely CB7 4HF
Tel: 01353 662062
tic@eastcambs.gov.uk

St. Mary's Church - Buckdon

Buckden Towers is famous as a residence of the Bishops of Lincoln from the middle of the 13th century to the 19th century. The first Vicar of the Church was

William de Bugden in 1217. It has carvings of animals around the porch. Open every day.

Buckden, Cambridgeshire
enquiries@stmarysbuckden.org.uk
www.ely.anglican.org/parishes/buckden
Getting there: Car - 30 minutes (22 miles) via A14.

The Manor

Built in the 1130s the Manor is one of the oldest continuously inhabited houses in Britain and much of the original house remains virtually intact over 900 years.

It was used during World War II by Lucy Boston to give gramophone record recitals twice a week to the RAF. The house is open by appointment only.

Hemingford Grey, Huntingdon, Cambridgeshire, PE28 9BN
Tel: 01480 463134
diana_boston@hotmail.com
www.greenknowe.co.uk
Open: Garden is open daily 11-5pm. House is open strictly by appointment only.
Admission: Adults - £7, Child £2.

Getting there: Car - 25 minutes (14 miles) via A14 westwards.

Wandlebury Country Park

Attractive parkland with woodland walks & a nature trail located within 5 miles of the city centre. 110 acres of woods and chalk grassland in the gentle Gog Magog Hills. A great place to wander with children. The grasslands are grazed by Texel sheep and Highland Cattle. Site of Iron Age hill fort. In the 17th century a racing stable was built inside the old hillfort for King James II.

There are many myths about the gods Gog and Magog. Some say they were buried nearby, and that on Fleam Dyke lies a golden chariot. Gervase of Tilbusy wrote a ghostly tale in 1219 that Wandlebury was ruled by a dark night-rider that no mortal could defeat. One day a brave Normal knight called Osbert took up the challenge and won.

There is a picnic site, marked walks and nature trail through woods. There is also a Banyard bird hide on the northern edge of Varley's Field, for watching wildlife.

Some hardened paths are buggy and wheelchair friendly. In autumn it is a great place to kick about in the leaves.

Wandlebury Ring, Gog Magog Hills, Babraham, Cambs CB22 3AE
Tel: 01223 243830
www.cambridgeppf.org/wandlebury-country-park
Open: from dawn until dusk every day.
Admission: Free

Getting there: Bus - Citiplus X13 towards Haverhill. **Car** - off the A1307 (£2.50 parking charge) 3 miles from Cambridge.

Wimpole Hall Estate

Built by Sir John Soane in 1794 for the 3rd Earl of Hardwicke, who was passionately interested in farming and agricultural improvement. The Home Farm and gardens have been producing vegetables, meat and eggs throughout the estates history and still do today. Best seen in summer. The gardens are Victorian, but much has now been modified.

The park, landscaped by Bridgeman, Brown and Repton, has lovely views, a Gothic folly and serpentine lakes. The garden has thousands of daffodils in April and colourful parterres in July and August. Note that buggies can't be taken into the main house. There are hip-carrying infant seats for loan, a children's guide and quiz/trail. It has a picnic area, cafe and children's play area.

Wimpole Hall, Arrington, Royston, Cambridgeshire SG8 OBW
Tel: 01223 206000
wimpolehall@nationaltrust.org.uk
www.nationaltrust.org.uk/wimpole-estate
Open: Feb – Nov - Daily 10:30-17:00. Hall: Park: Everyday dawn to dusk. Nov– mid Feb11:00-16:00.Park: Everyday dawn to dusk
Admission: Whole Property: Adult: £15.90 Child: £9.05, Family: £36.25; **Gardens only** £4.50, Child £2.25. **Farm OR Hall:** Adult: £9.05, Child £4.50

Getting there: Cycle - National Trust-permitted cycle path to entrance from Orwell (A603). **Car** - 8 miles SW of Cambridge off A603, Junc 12 of M11. **By Foot** - Wimpole Way from Cambridge.
Bus - Citi 2 towards Addenbrooks Hospital, get off on Cherry Hinton Road. 15 minutes from Cambridge Centre. **Train** - Arrington (1 mile)/Orwell (2 miles) Shepreth 5 miles. Taxi service from Royston 8 miles.

Around Cambridgeshire

Peterborough has ice skating, go karting and a steam train, or you can feed the ducks in a stroll through pretty **Ely**. Alternatively, visit **Houghton Mill** in Huntingdon, the **Horse Museum** in Newmarket. The picturesque medieval towns of **Saffron Walden**, **St Ives** and **St Neot's** are lovely.

Useful Websites

Children's Centres & Toy Librarys
www.cambridgeshirechildrenscentres.gov.uk
Children's Centres can offer advice and support for people with young kids. Some also have 'Toy Libraries' where you can lend toys for a small cost.

Education, Schools and Colleges
www.cambridgeshire.gov.uk/childrenandfamilies/education
There are 205 Primary Schools, 31 Secondary Schools and 24 Further Education Colleges state funded in Cambridgeshire.

BBC News Cambridgeshire
www.bbc.co.uk/news/England/cambridgeshire
Up to date news on the area, and weather reports.

Cambridgeshire County Council
www.cambridgeshire.gov.uk
Information on the County Council, housing, environment, jobs, families, policing and leisure. Check for education and childcare locally.

Cambridgeshire Net
www.cambridgeshire.net
Online community hub listing the details of thousands of local organisations such as venues for hire in Cambridgeshire.

CHATTERIS

Known for its Christmas lights which are funded by community donations. It also has a small museum and a good fish and chip shop (Petrou Brothers in West Park St).

Getting there: Car - 24 miles (45 minutes). **Train:** To Ely and then **Bus 9** to Chatteris, 1 hour total.

ELY

Ely (ee-lee) is a charming and historic place. It has a Georgian and medieval centre and pretty riverside walks running out into the fens around it. It is also one of the fastest-growing cities in Europe.

It's only 15 minutes by train from Cambridge. On a sunny day you can walk by the river, and see the ponies, ducks and geese. The Cathedral is the main attraction, and is quite spectacular.

You could also take a walk on the 'spy' trail, visit the old Gaol at the Museum, or join in the local festivities on Eel or Apple Day. There is a procession following an eel on Eel Day.

The odd name harks back to the days when Ely was an island ma-

rooned in the 'sea' of fens, which was full of eels. You can eat these eels locally to this day.

Getting there from Cambridge

Train - 15 minutes. **Bus** - 50 minutes (Stagecoach Bus 9 towards Chatteris). **Car** - 40 min's (17 miles) on the A10.

Getting Around

The railway station is about 10 minutes walk from the city centre, and there are frequent and reliable buses. There are long stay car parks outside the centre in Barton Rd, Fishermans, Newnham St and Ship Lane.

Ely Cathedral

This is a majestic sight, dominating the flat fens all around. It was built in 1082. The church is famous for its unique Octagon Tower and Lantern Tower which is floodlit at night. It is known as the 'ship of the Fens'.

Chapter House, The College, Ely CB7 4DL
www.elycathedral.org
Open: Summer: 09:00 – 17:00. Winter: 10:00 – 16:00. Access may be restricted during services and events.
Admission: Adults £8.00, Children under 12 free.

Stained Class Museum

This houses the national collection of British Stained Glass. The musem is on the upper level of Ely Cathedral up a short spiral staircase.

The South Triforium,
Ely Cathedral, Ely CB7 4DL
Tel: 01353 660347
info@stainedglassmuseum.com
www.stainedglassmuseum.com
Open: Summer Mon to Sat 10:30-5pm, Sun 12:00-4.30pm.
Admission: Adults £4.50 Under 16 free.

Ely Museum

A small museum located in the Bishops Gaol, with local history, Roman artefacts and a condemned cell.

The Old Gaol Market St, Ely CB7 4LS
Tel: 01353 666655
Open: Summer 10:30-17:00, Winter 10:30-16:00 (closed Tues), Mon - Sat. Sundays 13:00-16:00 or 17:00.
Admission: Adults £3.50, Children £1 (<5's free).

Jubilee Gardens

A lovely park by the riverside. It has a child's play area, sculptures, a bandstand and geese.

Jubilee Gardens Super Spy Trail

An interesting leaflet (see web site link) with a list of items for children to discover around the gardens. From the Ely Society.

www.elysociety.org.uk/index.php/walks

HUNTINGDON

Huntingdon grew up around a river crossing on the Great Ouse and was a staging post for Danish raids. Later, Dick Turpin was said to have been a visitor to the coaching inn here. Today, the Riverside Park is good place to watch boats pass by.

In Norman times, the town had sixteen churches but it declined after the Black Death. It was once the site of Huntingdon Castle built in 1068. This is now a public open space and is the site of the Castle Hills Beacon. The Manor (page 113) is nearby in Hemingford Grey.

Getting there: Car - 30 minutes (18 miles) on the A14 west. **Bus** - Citi 8 and then Busway B, 1 hour 10 minutes.

117

NEWMARKET

The headquarters of thorough bred breeding and training. If you get up very early you can see them train through the morning mist. It is a market town in Suffolk and has over 50 horse training stables and two large racetracks. It is also home to the Newmarket Sausage, a pork sausage from a traditional recipe.

Getting there from Cambridge

Train - 20 minutes. **Bus -** 40 minutes (Stagecoach Bus 11 towards Bury St Edmund's or 12 towards Ely). **Car -** 30 mins (18 miles) on A14 and then A142.

National Horseracing Museum

The stories and history of horse racing. You can try a horse simulator and dress up as a jockey.

99 High Street, Newmarket, Suffolk., CB8 8JH
Tel: 01638 667333
admin@nhrm.co.uk
www.nhrm.co.uk
Open: Monday to Sunday 10am to 5pm (closes at 4pm on Sundays)
Admission: Adults £6.50, Children (under 16 years) £3.50

Newmarket Racecourse

From the oldest race in history to the 21st Century, Newmarket hosts some of the world's top thoroughbred racing. Events include the Guineas Festival in May, the July Festival in high summer and the Future Champions Day in October.

Westfield House, The Links, Newmarket, Suffolk. CB8 0TG
Tel: 01638 675500
www.newmarketracecourses.co.uk

The National Stud

British Thoroughbred breeding. Set in 500-acres close to Newmarket, it opened its gates to the public for the first time in the mid-1970's. It remains the only working stud farm in the UK.

A tour will take you to the Foaling Unit and nursery paddocks where in the early spring, you may see a newborn foal. They take 90 minutes and you must pre book.

Wavertree House, The National Stud, Newmarket, Suffolk, CB8 0XE
Tel: 01638 663464
tours@nationalstud.co.uk
www.nationalstud.co.uk
Open: Tour times. Advised to arrive 15 mins befour tour starts. 14th February 2015 to 30th September at 11:15 am and 2:00 pm and from 1st October to 31st October at 11:15 am

Admission: Contact for details.Around £11 per person.
PRE BOOKING ESSENTIAL.

Cafes

Charlottes Tea Room and Bistro
3 High St, Newmarket CB8 8LX
Nice tea room with a view of the Clock Tower.

ROYSTON

Royston is very close by train from Cambridge. It is a reasonably sized market town with a museum, caves, an Arts Festival in October and nearby Wimpole Hall (see page 114). It is in Hertfordshire.

Getting there from Cambridge:

Train - 20 minutes. **Car -** 30 minutes (18 miles) o the A10.

Royston Museum

This contains the Royston Tapestry project, local history and a collection of ceramics and glass.

5 Lower King Street, Royston SG8 5AL
Tel: 01763 242587
www.roystonmuseum.org.uk
Open: Wed, Thur & Sat 10:00-16:45
Admission: Free

Royston Cave

This curious circular cave is hidden beneath the pavement. It is cut into the 60m (197ft) layer of chalk which underlies the town. Legend suggests that in the 13th century it was used as a secret meeting place by the Knights Templar. It has a range of wall carvings.

Melbourn Street, Royston
Tel: 01763 245484
www.roystoncave.co.uk
Open: Check website. Weekends Easter to September. Also open Wed in August.
Admission: Check website.

ST IVES

St Ives is 14 miles from Cambridge on the banks of the river Great Ouse. You can take the Guided Bus way there from Cambridge. It has a 15th Century Bridge and chapel over the river and is one of only three such surviving bridges in England. On the first and third Saturdays of each month an excellent Farmer's Market takes place.

Getting there

Bus - the Fens/the busway A towards Wyton Airfield (20 minutes) or busway B towards Hichingbrooke Park. **Car -** 25 minutes (14 miles) on A14 and A1096.

SAFFRON WALDEN

A picturesque, medieval town. Here you will find St Mary's Church, the largest parish church in Essex. Nearby, Saffron Walden Museum is one of the oldest purpose built museum buildings in the country, completed in 1835. It has everything from mammoth tusks to mummies, and the ruins of a Castle keep.

On the eastern side of Saffron Walden Common is the largest turf labyrinth still surviving in Eu-

rope. Children can follow 'path' through the turf, which winds for about one mile within a circle 100 feet (30.5 meters) in diameter.

For kids interested in skating and bikes, you can visit the One Minet Skate Park at the rear of Lord Butler Leisure Centre, Peaslands Road.

See Bridge End Garden which has seven interlinked gardens from the 19ᵗʰ Century. Also nearby is Audley End House.

Getting there from Cambridge

Train - 20 minutes towards London Liverpool Street, get off at Audley End and take the Bus 59 towards Haverhill (8 minutes). **Bus** - Citi 7 to Saffron Walden (10 hour 10 minutes). **Car** - 30 minutes (18 miles) on A11 then B184.

ST NEOTS

18 miles west of Cambridge, St Neots still retains its rich heritage. It dates back over 1000 years to the Medieval Priory of St. Neot. The name of the town comes from the Cornish saint.

It has a museum housed in the former magistrates court. It has a Lost Priory and you can walk in the footsteps of the famous 19th Century Eynesbury Giant.

The Riverside Mill and lock in Eaton Socon are also worth a look. Paxton Pits Nature Reserve is nearby with a wealth of wildlife.

Getting there from Cambridge

Car - 30 minutes via A428 (18 miles), **Bus** - Citi 1 and X5

PETERBOROUGH

Cathedral City 40 miles north of Cambridge. It is a large town but compact in the centre and has good public transport. You can take a trip on the steam engines at Nene Valley Railway, visit the Museum or go swimming in the Art Deco outdoor lido.

The Cathedral is the burial place of Katharine of Aragon, the first wife of Henry VIII. Five miles out of town is the interesting Flag Fen Archaeological Park.

Getting there:

Train - 50 minutes. **Bus** - National Express/350 1 hour 5 minutes. **Car** - 55 minutes (40 miles) on A14, A1 (M), A1139

Getting Around

Most of the city centre is pretty manageable on foot or with a buggy. It has a good range of car parks and public transport system. The cycle routes, or 'green wheel' are available in their Visitor Information Centre for £1.50. However you can also check out information on their website: www.travelchoice.org.uk

The buses are run by stagecoach. A family day ticket can be the cheapest option if travelling with children. It has citi 1 to 6 buses. Take the citi 3 to get to Planet Ice, and the citi 1 to get to the East of England Showground and Ferry Meadows.

The lovely steam train Nene Valley Railway runs through Ferry Meadows from the river by the city centre.

Attractions

Burghley House

An Elizabethan mansion with 18 state rooms and parklands designed by Capability Brown.

It now has a 'Garden of Surprises' with mirrors, water and sculptures.

Burghley Park Stamford, Lincolnshire PE9 3JY
Tel: 01780 752451
www.burghley.co.uk
Open: during the summer, check website for details.

East of England Showground

This has some of the biggest events in the region, including the East of England Show; Just Dogs Live; Equifest; Truckfest.

East Of England Agricultural Society, Peterborough PE2 6XE
www.peterborougharena.com

Ferry Meadows Country Park

A large 500 acre open area along the River Nene, through woodlands and meadow. There is a visitor centre, and also horse riding, fishing, sailing and boat trips.

Ferry Meadows, Ham Lane, Peterborough PE2 5UU
Tel: 01733 234193
www.neneparktrust.org.uk/ferry-meadows

Flag Fen Archaeological Park

This is a Bronze Age site with the oldest wheel in England and an ancient wooden track through the Fens. It is set in 37 acres of wild fenland and historic reconstructions.

There are regular events such as the bronze sword casting.

The Droveway, Northey Rd, Peterborough PE6 7QJ
Tel: 01733 313414
Parkinfo@flagfen.org
www.flagfen.org
Admission: Adult £5.00, Senior or Disabled Citizen: £4.50, Child £3.75, Children under 5 yrs free.

Getting there: Car - 1 hour 10 minutes (40 miles) on A10 then A1101. From Jct 5 of the A1139 turning at the Dog in the Doublet Pub. **Train** - 45 minutes towards Kings Lynn. 5 miles from Peterborough station.

Green Wheel

www.pect.org.uk
A network of cycle routes that circle the city with spokes leading to the centre.

 ## Nene Valley Railway

This is a heritage railway, with a Thomas the Tank Engine as well as other activities. It uses part of the original London and North Western line from Northamptonshire into the Cathedral city of Peterborough and the stations of Yarwell, Wansford, Ferry Meadows (Nene Park) and Orton Mere. Check website for open days. It is also worth checking the website to book Thomas Big Adventure and Santa specials.

There is a Museum, shop, cafe, Exhibition Engine Shed and Loco Yard. A 'Rover Ticket' allows unlimited travel on the day of purchase. Stations at Ferry Meadows in the heart of the 500 acre Nene Park, Orton Mere and Peterborough.

Eastern terminus of the Nene Valley Railway, Peterborough.
Tel: 01780 784444
nfo@nvr.org.uk
www.nvr.org.uk

Peterborough Museum

Recently improved with a £3.2 million grant, thousands of items in one of the city's most historic Georgian buildings.

Priestgate, Peterborough PE1 1LF
Tel: 01733 864663
peterborough.com
Open: Daily. Closed Mondays (open Bank holiday Mondays).
Admission: Free.

www.planet-ice.co.uk/arena/Peterborough
Admission: £10 with skate hire at the weekend. Family of 4 £34.00

Sacrewell Farm and Country Centre

Hidden away in a quiet valley setting near the A1, it has a restored Mill. There is a farm animal collection, restaurant and a play areas, walks and trails. You can tour the farm by tractor, feed the animals and meet Shire horses.

Thornhaugh, Peterborough PE8 6HJ
Tel: 01780 782254
info@sacrewell.org.uk
www.sacrewell.org.uk

Peterborough Cathedral

The Cathedral is one of the finest Norman buildings, and is a stunning place with a fine ceiling. It is especially atmospheric at Christmas time.

Minster Precincts, Peterborough PE1 1XS
Tel: 01733 355315
www.peterborough-cathedral.org.uk
Open: Mon-Fri 09:00-17:00, Sat 09:00-15:00, Sun 12:00-15:00
Admission: Free but donations are politely requested.

Planet Ice

A skating arena open daily with cafe. It has parent and toddler sessions on Sundays from 10:00-11:00.

1 Mallard Road, Peterborough PE3 8YN
Tel: 01733 260 222
pet.boxoffice@planet-ice.co.uk

Teamworks Karting Peterborough

Indoor high speed electric karting, open 7 days a week. This is one for the older kids who like speed and excitement!

4 Venture Park, Stirling Way, Peterborough PE3 8YD
Tel: 08451803020
info@teamworkskarting.com
www.teamworkskarting.com/peterborough

Annual Events

February

Anglesey Abbey Snowdrops
Anglesey Abbey, Cambridge
240 varieties of snowdrops to see, some originating at the gardens. This garden is fantastic all winter.

Lent Bumps - late Feb/early March
College bumps rowing race in lower river.

March

Cambridge Scie Festival
University of Cambridge
A fantastic event for the kids, there are hundreds of science events. Booking ahead advised.

Thriplow Daffodil Weekend
Celebration of the yellow flower!

April

Duxford Spring Air Show
Imperial War Museum, Duxford
Magnificent air shows and family events featuring World War aircraft.

Ely Eel Day
Centre of Ely
Procession with an Eel through Ely town, wth fun family activities.

May

Stilton Cheese Rolling
May Day Bank Holiday
Cheese Rolling has become an annual event in Stilton and every May Day in the main street teams do battle.

June

Arbury Carnival
Arbury Town Park, Campkin Rd, Cambridge
A carnival and family fun day out.

Hemingford Abbots Flower Festival
This vivid flower show is held every other year. The last one was in 2013.

Strawberry Fair - Cambridge
A popular event on Midsummer Common, with stalls and local bands.

July

Cambridge Shakespeare Festival
A seven week long event held in Cambridge Universities private gardens. A nice way to enjoy a picnic.

Flying Legends
Imperial War Museum, Duxford
One of the world's most celebrated air shows, full of thrills and nostalgia.

Godmanchester Gala
Godmanchester
This is an event held annually since the Queens Silver Jubilee. Open air concert picnic.

World Pea Shooting Championships
WitchamVillage Green
This annual competition and

village fair sees contestants from far and wide try their hand at pea shooting.

St Ives Carnival & Music Festival
Fun family activities.

Cambridge Folk Festival
Cherry Hinton Hall
One of the most famous folk festivals in the world. It is held in Cherry Hinton Hall site. Ry Cooder and Joan Armatrading have sung here.

August

Fenland Country Fair
Stow cum Quy Park
A traditional country fair. Usually vintage vehicles, sheepdog demos, falconry displays and more.

Milton Maize Maze
The Milton Maize Maze, Rectory Farm Shop, A10 Milton By-pass, Milton, Cambridge
July to September. In autumn the maize fields are burned into a huge maze which is great to get lost in.

September

Bridge the Gap Walk - Cambridge
The chance to visit Colleges while raising money for charity.

Cherry Hinton Festival
Cherry Hinton, Cambridge
A family fun day with music & activities.

Cambridge Film Festival
Hosted by the Arts Picturehouse, this is a good mix of films including children's.

Open Cambridge Weekend
Local residents get a chance to visit properties normally closed to the public.

Cambridge Dragon Boat Festival
River Cam
See the boats battle in this fun day out.

Stourbridge Fair
Stourbridge Common
Annual Recreation of the ancient fair. Stalls selling cheese, honey, medieval dancing and history talks.

October

Cambridge Festival of Ideas
University of Cambridge
Lots to think about! Many free events.

World Conker Championships
Oundle, Northamptonshire
Thousands flock to this market town to see the winner take the Conker Throne.

November

5th November - Bonfire Night
Cambridge - Midsummer Common
The annual bonfire and fireworks event.

December

Milll Road Winter Fair - Cambridge
The road is taken over with stalls and parade.

King's College Carols - Cambridge
24th December
Popular carol service, people queue for hours to get in.

ESSENTIAL (i) INFORMATION

**Emergency
fire/police/ambulance**
Tel: 999

**Cambridge City Council Housing
Advice**
Tel: 01223 457918

**Cambridge
Citizens Advice Bureau**
Tel: 0844 848 7979
www.cambridgecab.org.uk

Jobcentre Plus
Freephone 0800 055 6688

HEALTHCARE

NHS 111 service if you need medical help fast, but it's not a 999 emergency.

NHS Choices website
www.nhs.uk
This is a very useful website, you can look up local services, information, and even a symptom checker.

Addenbrooke's Hospital
Hills Road, Cambridge CB2 0DQ
General: 01223 235151
Accident & Emergency Telephone:
01223 217118

TRAVEL

AIR
Stansted Airport
Tel: 0870 0000303
www.stanstedairport.com
Stansted is London's third-busiest airport, 35 miles northeast of central London and the nearest to Cambridge. Direct trains to Cambridge; fast access to the M11.

BUS
Cambridge Coach Services
Tel 01223 236333
Stagecoach
Tel 01223 423554

Bus - Park & Ride
7 day a week service across five sites and parking is free. They are colour coded:
GREEN (Milton to Babraham Rd);
RED(Madingley Rd to Newmarket Rd)

National Express
Tel: 08717 818178
National Express operates from Parker's Piece to London, airports.

TRAIN
National Rail Enquiry Service
Tel: 08457 484950

TRAVEL INFORMATION
Traveline 0871 200 2233 -
Information on Bus, Train or ferry.

TAXI
Cambridge - Panther Taxis
Tel: 01223 715715

SUPPORT & ADVICE

Parenting

Barnardo's
www.barnardos.org.uk
Parenting support through family centres and work with children.

Family Advice
www.familylives.org.uk
A parenting charity with advice and information.

Parenting Support Centre
www.parenting.co.uk

Sticky Fingers Travel
www.stickyfingerstravel.com
Family friendly travel advice.

Single Parents

Cambridge UK Single Parents
www.facebook.com/CambridgeUkSingl
eParents

Gingerbread
www.gingerbread.org.uk

Support for Children

Childline
www.childline.org.uk
Tel: 0800 1111
Confidential information and advice for young people themselves on bullying, back to school and other topics.

NSPCC
National Society for the Protection of Children
www.nspcc.org.uk
Tel: 0808 800 5000
Text: 88858
Help@nspcc.org.uk
Help and advice if you are worried about a child, free 24 hour helpline.

Young Minds
www.youngminds.org.uk
Parent helpline: 0808 802 5544
Help and advice on young people's mental health and wellbeing.

Teenagers
Exams, Careers, Volunteering

UCAS Progress
www.ucasprogress.com
A website for 14-19 year olds to find courses and training in Cambridgeshire.

Youthoria - the website for 11-19 year olds in Cambridgeshire
www.youthoria.org
This informative website is packed with information for teenagers in Cambridgeshire. It includes job vacancies, news, features, apprenticeships, training, life advice, learning and more.

NHS Choices - Beat Exam Stress
www.nhs.uk/Livewell/childhealth6-15/Pages/Examstress
NHS website that has some handy tips on how to reduce exam stress. Getting good sleep, good food and exercising can help a great deal.

Healthy Teens

Physical Activity

Check out the activities listing in the swimming and sports section. There is a huge variety on offer and it has so many benefits for children and young people, it can improve mental wellbeing and physical fitness as well as reduce obesity.

The NHS recommends at least 1 hour of physical activity every day for children and young people, which should be a mix of moderate activity such as fast walking and vigorous activity like running. www.nhs.uk/Livewell/fitness/Pages/physical-activity-guidelines-for-young-people

Relationships

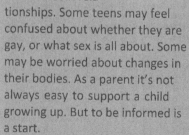

Teenagers are growing, maturing and at some point will take an interest in relationships. Some teens may feel confused about whether they are gay, or what sex is all about. Some may be worried about changes in their bodies. As a parent it's not always easy to support a child growing up. But to be informed is a start.

NHS Live Well - Teen Health

www.nhs.uk/Livewell/Sexandyoungpeople

Teenagers can find out about their health, how to stay safe, common myths about pregnancy, a bodies question and answer page, acne, bereavement, advice on how to avoid peer pressure, 'it's ok to say no' and other support.

Brook Advice Clinic

www.brook.org.uk

Confidential advice on sexual health for the under 25s.

Samaritans

24 hour telephone line: 08457 909090

www.samaritans.org

Talk to Frank

www.talktofrank.com

Confidential drugs advice.

Bullying

www.cambridgeshire.gov.uk/childrenandfamilies/parenting/childsbehaviour/bullying

The Cambridgeshire County Council website has useful information and advice. There are things that can be done to reduce or avoid bullying or being bullied. A child who avoids school, or becomes withdrawn, more anxious or aggressive may be experiencing bullying. You can also contact your child's school directly if you are at all concerned. See the section on computers for advice on online bullying.

Concern about Abuse

If you are concerned or suspect abuse, that a child may be suffering physical, sexual or emotional

abuse or neglect, or if as a parent or carer you feel that you may harm your child, then contact the Cambridgeshire Child Protection Team on 0345 045 5203 between 8am to 6pm Monday to Friday. Outside of these hours, the Emergency Duty Team is on 01733 234724 or the police 999.
Email:ReferralCentre.Children@cambridgeshire.gov.uk

The Team's website has more information on the signs of harm and what to do if you are at all concerned.
www.cambridgeshire.gov.uk/childrenandfamilies/parenting/keepingchildrensafe/childprotection/

You can also contact the NSPCC and young people can contact Childline (details in previous page).

Stop it Now!
Tel: 0808 10000 900
Help@stopitnow.org.uk
www.stopitnow.org.uk
A campaign to prevent child sexual abuse. It has a lot of advice and information.

Domestic Violence
Note: If you are being abused and are using a computer or phone to which your abuser has access, it is strongly recommended that you take measures to cover your activity, for example use a library or internet cafe.

Cambridge Domestic Violence Action Group
cambridgedomesticviolence.weebly.com

National Domestic Violence Helpline
Tel: (Freephone 24hr) 0808 2000 247

Cambridge Women's Aid
Tel: 01223 460 947
refuge@cambridgewa.org.uk
www.womensaid.org.uk
Information, support and temporary accommodation.

Mankind
Tel: 01823 334 244
www.mankind.org.uk
Support for male victims of domestic abuse and domestic violence

Refuge
www.refuge.org.uk
Help for women and children facing domestic violence.

Technology and Kids
Have you ever wondered how much time to let your kids play computer games, watch TV, or whether to get an Ipad?

Kids naturally want to keep up with other kids. So what limits, if any, should you choose? There is also the cost consideration, you can't get your kid the latest phone if you have not got the money.

However there are other concerns, such as bullying online, exposure to inappropriate material, children's lack of exercise from sitting around, and spending excessive hours playing the Xbox. Generally, the information that I've read recommends that you talk to your child about online dangers, and tell them what to do if they are worried. Explain that anything they put online could be seen by anyone, and it is important not to pass on detailed information such as their name, age or address. Use filtering software to block inappropriate sites and get to know and understand what websites they visit.

Microsoft recommends that up to at least the age of 10 years you should sit with your children while they use computers. As they go into the teens, to continue to supervise their activities, educate them about safe use and set clear rules. Keep the computers where you can see them rather than their bedrooms.

Here are some sources of information to help you protect your child and make up your own mind about what limits to set.

Childline - Advice for Children - Online Bullying
Tel: 0800 1111
www.childline.org.uk/Explore/Bullying/Pages/online-bullying

NSPCC Keeping Your Child Safe Online
www.nspcc.org.uk/help-and-advice/for-parents/keeping-your-child-safe

Microsoft Age-based Guidelines for Kids' Internet Use
www.microsoft.com/en gb/security/family safety/childsafety-age

Think U Know
www.thinkuknow.co.uk
Website for kids about online safety.

Online Fun and Games for Kids

Cbeebies
www.bbc.co.uk
Toddler TV, education, fun & games from the BBC.

CBBC
www.bbc.co.uk/cbbc
Children's TV, education and fun.

Guinness World Records
www.guinnessworldrecords.com

Haring Kids
www.haringkids.com
Interactive site with online colouring and animation.

How Stuff Works
www.howstuffworks.com
Informative, interesting website that will widen your child's world.

Acknowledgements & Credits

Index

If you like this book, there are more in the series...

Cambridge with Kids: The Essential Guide for Families

This is a larger, colour version of this Pocket Guide. In addition, it includes a large listing of childcare, sports and arts activity providers.

There's so much to do locally, from wildlife parks to adventure and activity centres, and it's all listed in one handy book. The book is packed with full colour photo's from around the area, and in easy to use sections.

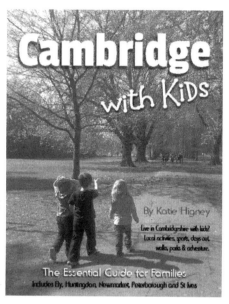

Brighton with Kids: The Family Guide

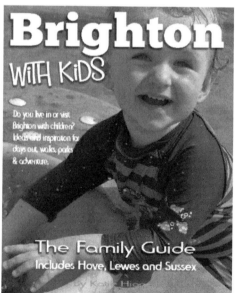

Whether you live in Brighton or Hove, or are visiting the area, this book is full of ideas and inspiration for days out. It is in full colour with photographs and maps. It also has sections on Lewes, Sussex and a day out in London. Wildlife, gardens, historic places, playgrounds, local attractions and walks.

Buy these from Amazon or other outlets.

134

Printed in Great Britain
by Amazon.co.uk, Ltd.,
Marston Gate.